SURELY THE GODS LIVE HERE

AN INCREDIBLE JOURNEY TO THE HIMALAYAS AND SIKKIM

SURELY THE GODS LIVE HERE

BY DAVID LANK

ILLUSTRATED BY THE AUTHOR

The Brownstone Press
1982

Published by
The Brownstone Press Limited
34 King Street E., Suite 510, Toronto
Canada M5C 1E5

Designed by David Lank and Don Fernley
Edited by Cathy Munro

Canadian Cataloguing in Publication Data

Lank, David M., 1937-
   Surely the gods live here
ISBN 0-919275-30-3 (Trade)
ISBN 0-919275-32-X (Limited Ed.)
1. Sikkim (India) - Description and travel.
2. Hiking - India - Sikkim. I. Title
DS 485.S52L36   915.4'1670452   C82-094120-4

Printed and bound in Canada.
Distributed by John Wiley & Sons Canada Ltd.

CONTENTS

"We will go up into the Hills – the high
hills – up to the sound of snow-water
and the sound of the trees."

RUDYARD KIPLING, *Kim*

For Ellen and Peter, and the rest of the base camp, but especially for Gillian and Mickey who shared all that is recorded in these pages.

PREFACE

Folded into the hidden valleys of the Himalayas lies Sikkim. Until very recently it was an independent kingdom wedged between the Indian state of West Bengal and the Kingdom of Bhutan. To the west lies Nepal; to the north lies China and its Tibetan territories. Directly south, beyond the foothills, stretches the dusty furnace of the Gangetic Plain. At different times and in different places, Sikkim has assumed very different sizes and shapes on world maps, but maps reflect realpolitik. A small, isolated, and by twentieth century standards a backward, almost medieval state which finds itself strategically located cannot expect to endure independently. Sikkim did not. It became a protectorate of India in 1950, the monarchy was abolished in a referendum of April 1975, and Sikkim was formally made the twenty-second state of the Indian Union in May, 1975. The process of dismemberment started by the British in the 1850s, when half the country was taken away, was completed by those same Indians who so detested British imperialism.

Despite now being an integral part of a modern state, Sikkim remained as it had been for centuries basically off limits. It was this very isolation that first attracted us. The tales of mass trekkings and mass trekkers in neighbouring Nepal were not to our liking. Perhaps fewer than 100 westerners had ever set foot in the area that we were to penetrate. The trek would cross several floral and faunal zones from tropical valleys to eternal snow and would pass through one of the world's greatest remaining cloud forests. We would be in vast rhododendron forests and would climb jungle trails lined with hundreds of species of wild orchids. The bird life would be spectacular, and above all, the leech season would be over by the time we arrived. In this tiny state, no bigger than Delaware (or, as someone quipped, as big as Australia if you flattened it out), opportunities still existed to experience ancient mountain cultures for which politics held no meaning.

It would also test the physical limits of some basically healthy but untrained city folk. The degree of difficulty was listed as Grade B-2, officially defined "below 15,000 feet, and moderate." We ended up well above 15,000 feet, and some of the veteran trekkers claimed it was very strenuous compared to other 'moderate' trips they had taken in the Himalayas.

Certainly one of the most powerful attractions of the whole trip was that this represented an exciting expedition within the physical reach of ordinary people. As it turned out, the trip exceeded our every wish.

I have chosen to write this story along lines inspired by the travel books of the nineteenth century, where the human factor adds flesh and breathes life into an otherwise dry skeleton of facts and figures. The bulk of the text is based – in many cases verbatim – on the extensive diary that I kept during the trip. After the passage of time, events that took place on the trip assumed new meaning as they were viewed in new contexts. I have tried to interpret these while at the same time attempting to keep the intimacy of the actual moments. As would be expected, such a trip stimulated me to learn a lot more about the country, its people, traditions, history, geography, geology, weather, flora and fauna. Where relevant, I have inserted facts and explanations that will be of special interest to trivia buffs.

But somewhere I have to draw the line, heedful of the delightful quote attributed to John Murray, the great publisher of countless early books on travel and science by Charles Darwin, Henry Bates, Dr. Livingstone, Austin H. Layard and many others. He cautioned Sir Charles Lyell, author of the pivotal *Principles of Geology*: "The more complete you make your book, Lyell, the fewer I shall sell of it." Some of the illustrations were done from life during the trek itself. The others were based either on the field sketches or were aided by some of the more than 1000 slides that were taken.

The text and pictures offer a taste of an incredible part of the world served not by a mountaineer but rather by one of your neighbours.

There are three main characters, all from Montreal: Gillian McConnell, a fashion designer, originally from Manchester, England; Micheline "Mickey" Wilson, an executive in a family heavy machinery firm; and myself, a partner in an investment counselling firm. Though fit, we were in no better shape than anyone who leads a fairly active and athletic life. Jogging, tennis, scuba diving, skiing and, in my case, ice hockey were our main forms of exercise. Mickey and I had on separate occasions been at altitudes over 13,000 feet in the Andes, and Gill had climbed Mount Inyangani in Zimbabwe. All of us had skied in the Alps frequently above 11,000 feet. While none of us had had any training specifically related to Himalayan trekking up to, according to the brochure, 15,000 feet, we had no reason to expect that we would have undue difficulty.

In addition, we had wonderful encouragement and support from many people. First and foremost were Gillian's husband, Peter, and my wife, Ellen, who chose to stay at home to attend to family and business matters, relieving us of all concerns on these fronts for the three weeks we would be away. Mickey's family was well equipped to manage in her absence as all her children were grown. Friends were lavish in their help during the preparatory stage. Dr. Jim Sullivan, an orthopedic surgeon with a side specialty in sports medicine as a doctor for the Canadian Olympic and Pan-American Games Teams, created our portable hospital, and was with us vicariously on the trip that he had originally planned to share. His wife, Janice, had trekked with Mickey in South America, and gave much time and thought to the outfitting. Marlene Foch and Kate Reed, both of Montreal, and intrepid trekkers in Nepal, gave many helpful tips. Herb Grossman of Mountain Travel of Albany, California, and his colleagues were of inestimable help in organizing the actual trip. I also want to give an unsolicited testimonial to Wood's Bag and Canvas. Their down-filled jackets and sleeping bags were the envy of our fellow trekkers from around the world. We wore Tyrol hiking boots with a three-quarter metal shank. Once the boots were broken in, they were marvellously comfortable. Despite what proved to be deplorable conditions, we never suffered from wet feet. The boots were without doubt the most important piece of equipment.

Special homage has to be paid to the memory of the late Eric Shipton whose cherished friendship, born while climbing together in the Galapagos Islands, inspired me to learn more about the mountains of the world. It was Eric who had led the first Himalayan climbs in which a then young New Zealander, Edmund Hillary, took part. There was also a young sherpa on Eric's climb named Tenzing. We had met Sir Edmund during two of his visits to Montreal in connection with the wonderful humanitarian work of his Foundation which has built many schools and hospitals for the mountain people in Nepal. Trekking in Sikkim with Mountain Travel would afford us the fulfilment of a dream: to meet Tenzing, thereby enabling us to pay our respects to three of the men who had had so much to do with the climbing of Everest.

And lastly, a word of special thanks for the long-suffering support and encouragement from my partner, Hamish Macaulay, who minded the store while I was off, yet again, on another trip. Hamish had climbed several important peaks in the Himalayas and in the St. Elias Range in northern Canada. His tips, from the personal experience of an expert, were of inestimable value.

DML
Town of Mount Royal
August 1981

INTRODUCTION

Around Christmas, 1978, we decided that a trip to the Himalayas would be a fine idea. Two years later, our base camp wished us a fond farewell at an unforgettable dinner, highlighted by a giant cake sculptured in the form of a mountain peak, complete with snow, a dozen or so HO gauge sherpas and porters carrying packs made of painted raisins, a matchstick bridge with a lace railing over a stream, and a tiny Canadian flag.

Had we been superstitious, the trip would by then have long since been cancelled. We had contacted Mountain Travel in Albany, California, and had received the brochures, forms and instructions on inoculations and impedimenta. Applications for trekking permits were filled out in triplicate, and six passport photos were dispatched via first class mail to California on the first of August. India, consistent with an approach to the twentieth century that we would later come to know, needed six weeks to process the applications, all of which had to be submitted as part of a group application. Without any information, the deadline came and went. (The originals finally arrived in California six weeks later.) The situation was rapidly becoming desperate. Endless letters and phone calls turned "Dear Mr. Grossman" of Mountain Travel into "Dear Herb." On his suggestion, we made copies of the originals that had been kept in Montreal, had six more pictures taken, and direct contact was established with the High Commission for India in Ottawa.

I had the unique experience of dealing with the Indian government. "The whole business of talking to these guys is a hand-wringing experience," Herb had warned. What to us was an obvious situation – that the original requests for the visas had been lost in the mail, that we were part of a group the full particulars of which were supplied, that time was breathing down our necks – fell on the totally uncomprehending and unsympathetic ears of the minor official in charge of visas.

He was not the slightest bit interested in furthering our cause. "Much of the money will be spent here, not in India," was his factual if somewhat stupid answer to our inquiry (voiced in increasing frustration and even desperation) as to whether or not he was interested in helping us spend tourist dollars in his own country. He insisted that the six week requirement for processing requests could not possibly suffer from "deviation," even though the officially required elapsed time would produce approval two weeks *after* we were scheduled to be in Darjeeling. In a hand-wringing rage I demanded to speak to the First Secretary. "I do not want you to speak with him," said the minor official. "And remember that I can procrastinate and ensure that you will not arrive at all. I have the power to interfere." The First Secretary apologized profusely for the unacceptable behaviour of the official and, upon promising to take the whole matter under his personal attention, heard the whole story over again. All that would be needed, he said, was a list of everyone in the group, their addresses and passport numbers and the exact itinerary that we intended to follow. To an Indian civil servant, perhaps a simple and logical request. Just send the above, along with six passport photos and the three legal size applications in triplicate, and he would forward everything to Delhi. There would be absolutely nothing to worry about because he personally would send a covering telegram.

On Wednesday, everything was completed, and was sent overnight by courier service to the High Commission where it arrived at 9 A.M. Thursday. The diplomatic pouch left for Delhi at 11 A.M.; our official, who had intercepted the precious documents, had delivered them to his superior exactly one hour too late.

"Why didn't you tell me you needed them by a certain time?" I pleaded. "I would gladly have brought the papers to Ottawa myself yesterday afternoon!" With an undeniable ring of logic, the official's superior pointed out that it would not be wise for the Indian government to announce the schedule of their diplomatic pouches. The next one would be leaving in a week, scant consolation in view of the fact that we now had only three weeks left in which to cram six weeks of bureaucratic bumbling.

"Could you send everything to New York for their next pouch?" I asked.

There was a pause, an audible change in the man's breathing, and then a slow, metered accusation: "How did you know that there would be a diplomatic pouch from New York?"

"The United Nations . . ." I started to explain, but his suspicions had been aroused. It is a peculiar conceit of Third World countries that their officials base all their actions or inactions on the assumption that everyone is a spy who can hardly wait to map their land while disguised as butterfly collectors or whatever prior to launching a full invasion. The memories of "The Great Game" live on other than just in the pages of Kipling and Flashman.

"Never mind," snapped the official. "I will send a telex with the next pouch to expedite the matter." This being my first experience with Indian officialdom, I took him at his word. At what a disadvantage are we who act in good faith on the word of an official! As it was, he completely ignored our visa applications, sent not a word by telex and was suddenly unavailable by phone. When I finally got through to him two weeks later, he had completely forgotten about our case, but assured us that there would be no problem. We thought a phone call to California would help, but the reply there was, "Herb Grossman is out of the country, but he'll be back in three weeks. What trip? Oh, well, I'll see if someone here knows anything about it."

One of Herb's assistants found the file, and in it was a recently received copy of a letter from Daku Norgay, the agent in Darjeeling (whom we would come to know and love), which she had sent to Delhi with our names, addresses and passport numbers included in the group request. It did seem that we would have no difficulty getting into a country which was notoriously difficult to get into. Although we did not have the final confirmation in hand, we decided to risk it and leave on schedule.

The tetanus, typhoid and yellow fever shots had changed from pure pain to immunization. Mickey had wrenched her shoulder practising for the trek on Vermont's Mount Mansfield, but now the shoulder was strong enough to go. Blisters had turned into callouses on our feet after forced marches on Mount Royal in the new climbing boots.

A week before leaving, we checked out the sleeping bags, down jackets, endless packets of fruit crystals, balaclavas and booties bought during several shopping expeditions to the Army Navy Surplus Store. The portable hospital was divided up, and the packing was given a dry run. A large duffle bag, a 270cc JanSport knapsack, and a small rigid lockable case were all the luggage each of us would have to carry the clothing, trekking gear, cameras, lenses and films (we would return with over a thousand slides), boots, sleeping bags and quantities of ball point pens that we would be handing out to smiling, quaint natives along the easy trail in exchange for their priceless trinkets.

October 3, 1980 dawned in a blanket of fog, still without any word from India on the fate of our visas. At 6:15 in the morning we met at the Eastern Airlines counter at Dorval to catch the first flight out of Montreal to New York. The earliness of the hour, and the fact that it was not Air Canada would, we hoped, minimize the delays that would be caused by the wildcat strike of the air traffic controllers.

And this is where the Diary begins.

SURELY THE GODS LIVE HERE

THE DIARY

All of our contingency plans were unnecessary – the drive to New York by bus, the overnight train or a flight out of Burlington to La Guardia – as Eastern took off on the appointed day at 7:45 A.M., a mere 40 minutes late despite the strike of the controllers. We joined hands as we lifted off, starting on an adventure into the unknown. We had read the brochures, and had talked to friends, but none of us really felt that we knew what we were in for. A full day in New York would be a welcome transition. We had a 6 P.M. deadline at Air India at John F. Kennedy International Airport. For a 7:30 flight, an hour and a half leeway would surely allow us to get good seats. However, all the window seats had long since been spoken for by the time we arrived. With the passage of countless eastern minutes slipping by with only the westerners becoming agitated, it became increasingly obvious that the "delayed" departure meant that the flight had not even left London. Equally obvious was the fact that we were going to miss every connection in what was already a very tight – too tight – schedule. In a sincere attempt to be helpful, the ticket agent sought us out, and handed us re-issued tickets for a later flight to Delhi and Bombay. Our bags, of course, had been checked through to Calcutta on the continuation of the original flight. A mini-scene convinced the agent to allow us to get our bags unloaded from the containers so that they could be re-ticketed to Bombay with us. The scheduled flight to Delhi was out, and the best they could do was to offer a "requested on the first available flight." "Perhaps in two or three days," was the agent's answer to the inevitable question. We were not alone. Virtually all our fellow passengers and their families and friends were lined up behind the single routing agent whose vapid smile emphasized her towering incompetence. There was plenty of time to pace the endless corridors as the hours dragged on. Finally, we were herded like not-so-sacred cattle onto the 747 for a departure at 1:40 A.M. and promptly ran into the worst turbulence I have ever experienced in a large commercial aircraft. From our three middle seats in the centre section right at the back of the plane we had the benefits of all the fish-tailing that the structural engineers could have foreseen in the testing of the airframe. A trayful of Bloody Marys floated through the cabin and landed in the lap of the Californian accountant sitting next to me. "Oy! That's service! How did they know I love Bloody Marys!" A lady came out of the aft toilet, and flew through the air with the greatest of screams, landing heavily in the aisle. The public address system called for a doctor while she was being strapped into her seat. The atmosphere was heightened by screaming children.

We slept fitfully before eating a truly atrocious breakfast of baked brick omelette. Things a travel agent doesn't tell you about Air India. And if you go standby, it's cheaper than Icelandic, and there are usually plenty of seats as far as London. The main crush gets on in London, known to some as the third largest city in India, and the second largest in Pakistan.

Heathrow, as always, was a madhouse. The plane was delayed another two hours, finally getting off at 2:40 P.M. London time. The newcomers from London got all the window seats, and so we missed all of Europe. Getting up for a stretch we could catch a glimpse of the Jura and the Alps. A truly awful Sophia Loren movie with endless flaming crashes and ludicrous plot took up an hour, and mercifully put out all the lights. Flying time estimated at eight and a half hours, longer than usual as the route had to avoid flying over Iran/Iraq. No one seemed to have any idea what time it was – 3:10 P.M. Montreal time, 8:10 London time, and ?:?? Air India time. At around 4 A.M. local time, we began to lose altitude, and the Indians sleeping in the aisles in lotus positions began to stir themselves. At midnight London time and 4:35 A.M. Bombay time we touched down. It was 27°C. Even if the temperature had been listed as 91° Fahrenheit, it could not have seemed more oppressively, steamingly, wiltingly hot. We were escorted under armed guard to the immigrations and baggage area to claim our belongings which were nowhere to be seen. The harassed Air India agent disappeared with our baggage stubs, and we were left to ponder our fate during a sauna-like bus ride through back roads within the airport confines. In spite of the darkness, we could see all manner of human activity by the flickering, smoking fires of the hovels of the squatters who had brought the tenth and the twentieth centuries right along the run-ways. People singly and in groups glided along as silently as bats, with a shadowy form sliding across the road in front of us like a dark weasel. The grinding and complaining of the bus drowned out all the night noises, but the air, despite the best efforts of our fellow passengers to compete, hung heavy with the perfume of dung fires with a hint of human excrement. And our bags – and baggage stubs – would probably never again be seen. Five or so kilometers later we were discharged in the transit lounge of the new but already decrepit domestic terminal. We lined up in total confusion at a make-shift ticket counter where two flights to Delhi were being processed interchangeably.

Bored passenger
on Air India

A shriek from Gillian brought everything to a full stop; an immense rat emerged from under the bench, and was check-ing out her knapsack. Welcome to Bombay! Only the Indians seemed totally unconcerned. Despite feeling that death by thirst was imminent, we ignored the large arrow pointing to "Drinking Water" above a fountain not too far from where the rat had been seen last. Behind an attendant-less counter,

"welcome to Bombay"

Mus rattus

bottled soft drinks beckoned cruelly. Someone finally showed up, and we drank deeply of mango juice, "Thumbs-up Cola," Limca – a lemon-lime type of drink – and some concoction of sarsaparilla.

The sun burst up through steaming thunderheads and our first Indian morning was full-blown upon us. Dozens of house crows – our first Indian bird – converged from the tall grasses and surrounding buildings on our stifling lounge, insinuating their way through gaps in grey corrugated tin walls onto the erector-set beams that held up the roof and gave support to the completely ineffectual Humphrey Bogart fans suspended everywhere. The crows, with an occasional sinister caw, hopped from strut to strut with complete contempt for the humanity that had built their jungle bars. Gillian and Mickey called them "revolting," a sentiment not shared by Frank Oatman whom we met. He had worked with the ornithologist Irby Davis in Austin, Texas on assorted bird books, and was on his way to Sri Lanka via Nepal (to visit the Flemmings, renowned Himalayan ornithologists) to lead a bird watchers' trip. It was Oatman who pointed out the Intermediate Egret that flapped across the tarmac in front of the building. (Trivia time: tarmac should be spelled "Tarmac" with a capital because it is a trademark which combines "tar" and "macadam," itself named after the Scottish inventor of the macadamized road first introduced in the United States between Philadelphia and Lancaster in 1794.)

In the otherwise perfectly flat landscape of the airport, the only relief was a substantial dump, a magnet for scores of pariah kites. They wheeled and circled, and then slipping air they sailed low on gliding wings before dropping abruptly to their fetid feast. The common house sparrow here is replaced by the Eurasian tree sparrow, and they were everywhere. Egrets and a paddy bird, a shrike, and mynahs were all duly

Common Pariah Kite
Milvus migrans

noted to the bemused incomprehension of the slovenly civil police who sat around looking positively silly in their plastic shoes, shorts, and double thickness greenish khaki wool leggings up to their calves. They also could not understand why anyone would be interested in a fist-sized locust, and a beautiful chestnut coloured butterfly with lustrous eyes on the wings – a *Melanitis leda*, our first Indian insect. Of course, we were not allowed to take any photos, because the transit lounge was of great military significance. House crows perched a wing-flap apart all over the tail and radio vanes of a 747; too bad, it would have made a nice picture.

By 7:15 local time (i.e. 7:15 October 5, or 9:45 P.M. on October 4 back in Montreal) the world of the squatter hordes was in full swing. Beggars, scrapers, a woman in a sari balancing a beaten water jug of breathtaking symmetry on her head, our first sacred cows, a goat on the runway, children washing in swamp water and everywhere house crows and pariah kites. Hovels hugged the runway, people were everywhere and the squalor was beyond comprehension. We could see all this from the bowed windows of our jet. Finally, at 8 A.M. with new baggage checks and blind faith in hand, we took off for Delhi. Out over the ocean, fishing boats anchored near their home villages over a vast green flood plain drained by meandering ribbons of streams and tide water. We all wanted to watch, but the curry breakfast and the confused hours we had just spent overcame us. We slept until a noticeable change in altitude announced our impending arrival more closely than either the English or Hindi message announced over the speaker. The ground below was now very arid, clumps of vegetation linked by dusty tracks. Following the most convoluted flight path, we wove an unseen labyrinth through the air towards the Delhi airport – a path chosen, no doubt, to confuse hostile aircraft that must surely be following us in. Outside Delhi was a splendid ruin of a fort with battlements so huge they looked more like a geologic outcropping than anything that could possibly be man made. Nearby, man and erosion combined to honeycomb upthrustings of baked earth with wells that must have been as old as time. Like so many ants, labourers were turning mud into brick, while unseen, others were disembowelling the stacks, creating a landscape of black holes surrounded by doughnuts of detritus. It was absolutely Biblical.

We had been flying at only fifteen hundred or so feet for quite awhile, low enough to see and identify hundreds of Egyptian and black vultures. Many actually flew above us. And then we landed in Delhi. The air-conditioned cabin was overwhelmed by the 33°C furnace that blasted through the door. Our documents were checked by three sets of officials, one of whom lost none of his accusative surliness while reading my passport upside down. To clear customs and to claim the baggage we were handed bronze tablets with raised letters and numbers. Each tablet must have weighed a quarter of a pound, and would have made a kleptomaniac's mouth water. In India snatching a customs tablet is probably punishable by lopping off a hand.

With an endless wait for baggage in front of us, I decided to seek approval to photograph the one bird that we had jokingly never thought we would ever see. On the way across the Atlantic and across another quarter of the world, I had been studying Salim Ali's *Field Guide To The Birds Of The Eastern Himalayas*. The vast majority of birds and their families were unfamiliar to me. On the dust jacket was a series of drongos, the only bird that Gillian now knew. On landing at Delhi she blithely mentioned that "Over there, there's a drongo sitting on the scaffolding." And damn it, there was! To photograph a drongo at an airport meant, unavoidably,

Our first Indian butterfly,
Melanitis leda.
Bombay, October 4, '80

19

photographing the airport, which, of course, is totally forbidden. Three sets of officials had to be contacted before permission was finally received. An armed escort was provided. This all took time, but the bags had not yet been delivered.

Mickey and Gill took the tickets and had them rewritten for that night's Calcutta flight while I took the bags to the luggage check. As two of the knapsacks were not locked, an underling wove a spiderweb of stout cord through every eyelet and strap, finishing off, under the stern eye of his superior, with a blob of smoking sealing wax.

Then to stand in line to change some dollars and travellers' cheques into rupees. In the dingiest of money-changer's cubicles, three officials took their time shuffling papers. As I inched forward, I discovered that the reason for their speed was the need to copy by hand every serial number of every bill and cheque into a ponderous ledger. These entries were then checked by a government overseer who re-copied the same numbers into his own ledger. The exchange was calculated on a trip-bar machine of great historic interest, before another overseer mentally recalculated everything before issuing a piece of paper that had to be presented at another wicket at the end of another line. Careful checking of passport numbers and comparing of signatures then ensued before a stack of rupees was stuffed through the grate. It took one hour.

With hours to kill, we engaged a taxi for a tour of the city with, as it turned out, the most truly awful taxi driver in the subcontinent. Gill kept on trying to get him to drive us through "the slums," or, in her Manchester accent, "the slooms." The tour, we agreed, would cost 140 rupees. Being Sunday, everything was closed, but we drove past endless brick developments which, the driver kept insisting, were homes for the MPs. If this were really one of the fringe benefits of being a Member of Parliament, then political life could hold little attraction. They were real slums. It later dawned on us that "MPs" were the Military Police, whose name was legion.

The streets and vacant lots were lined with cities of mud and tents. Sacred cattle abused their rights everywhere. The dean of Canada's bird artists, Terence Shortt, once described a similar scene, "Great upwellings of stink," in his book. Vultures stared humpbacked from every tree. The smoke from the cooking fires cast a haze and everywhere was the inescapable heat. New brick apartment buildings were scaffolded with rickety but apparently extremely strong bamboo.

We pulled up in front of the key hole entrance to a reddish and dilapidated version of the Taj Mahal, identified by the driver as the "Tombs of Delhi." A face appeared from the pitch black window of a room imbedded in the massive walls. Three tickets were issued along with the unmistakable stench of human urine. Time, the climate and the lack of upkeep had been unkind to what once must have been a remarkable structure. Distance was kind; on not-too-close inspection it was plain that everything was flaking off. A guided tour through the dank corridors disturbed some bats that squeaked from one roost to another, but outside this oasis of green added a dozen birds to the life list. Yellow-wattled plovers strutted stiff-leggedly by the 'tank' whose stagnant green scum was dimpled by countless water bugs. A flock of Alexandrine parrots screeched by to lose themselves in the drooping fronds of a large palm. A score or more of large grey babblers earned their name, arguing over every crevice in the crumbling walls. Swallows, swifts, house crows, tree sparrows and mynahs added their noises to the incessant buzzing of unseen cicadas. Three pot-smoking men tried to get Gill to pay for the right to photograph "their

Sacred snooze – Delhi

1. White-backed Vulture - *Gyps bengalensis*
2. Scavenger Vulture - *Neophron percnopterus*
3. Pariah Kite - *Milvus migrans*
4. Red-wattled Lapwing - *Vanellus indicus*
5. Large Grey Babbler - *Turdoides malcolm*
6. Common Mynah - *Acridotheres tristis*
7. Black Drongo - *Dicrurus adsimilis*
8. Alexandrine Parrakeet - *Psittacula eupatri*
9. House crow - *Corvus splendens*
10. Jungle crow - *Corvus macrorhynchos*
11. House Swift - *Apus affinis*

Birds seen in Delhi

22

sacred cow." A striped ground squirrel scurried from shade to shade. Overhead a hundred or more kites and vultures wheeled on the thermals that welled up like transparent versions of the onion-domed architecture of the tombs. It was so hot that breathing was difficult.

Our taxi had attracted a small crowd of street vendors, and a charmer whose reluctant cobra kept slithering back under the folds of his coat despite or perhaps because of the wailing flute. Off to the Emporium to look at display cases full of uncut and unmounted stones, silks, cottons, inlaid table tops and a vast array of tackiness. Peacock fans were more tempting, really, than the out of focus Kamasutra postcards.

It was too hot to continue, so off to the Hotel Lohti via Washington-like malls with every spot of shade taken by family groups or dancing bears. We arrived at the Lohti despite at least two attempts by the driver to take us to one of the hotels he had a special deal with. We finally arrived with 49 rupees showing on the meter. I paid 100, and told him he was a thief for trying to negotiate 150 from an unsuspecting tourist. He followed us into the blessedly air-conditioned lobby to press his case until chased out by a large, pyjama-clad doorman.

Assuring the desk clerk that I alone would be making use of the day room, I signed in, and slipped Mickey and Gill the key. The only furniture was a single bed. We had now been up for 60 hours straight, and this was no time for prudishness. We stripped to whatever level decency would allow, and the three of us collapsed on the bed. We slept like dead men before taking a taxi back to the airport through the gathering dusk, joining an unbelievably wild traffic jam of cars, bicycles, rickshaws, cattle and a seething mass of humanity interspersed with the smoke and smell of countless cooking fires of the family territories staked out along the sidewalks. What

is the attraction of this place? And this is meant to be the least horrific of the three main cities! Whole families set off from their neighbours by billowing veils and shrouds, with only holy men and beggars passing from territory to territory. Human beasts of burden carry unthinkable loads of every description, towering cargos of faggots and straw. Sacred cows all over the road, and a cacophony of horns that gives every driver the right of way regardless of red lights. The confusion at the airport was, if possible, even greater.

The plane was of course late. We retrieved our bags, confirmed that the sealing wax was still intact, were frisked through customs and security and sat down to wait in the transit lounge. We all agreed that it would have been physically impossible to do what we had done had we been more than, say, five people. It simply would have taken too long to handle the bags, the money and the rewriting of the tickets for more people than that. And while we were thinking about this, we watched several small mice rummaging through the display case of cheap souvenirs. I did, however, buy a copy of another Salim Ali bird book, and penned in the twenty new names from today. We were off to Calcutta so that we could catch the flight tomorrow to Bogdogra, then by car to Darjeeling to catch up with our group. The flight for Calcutta was announced, and as we were filing in, another flight was listed as ready to receive passengers: a direct flight to Bogdogra. No one had bothered to tell us. It was a lesson we should have remembered. The next piece of culture shock was only minutes away.

None of us smokes, and as we are really inconvenienced by smoke on aircraft, we asked to be put in the nonsmoking section of the A-300 Airbus of Indian Airlines. The smiling ground hostess gave us seats 2A, B and C. As soon as the No Smoking sign went off, everyone in rows 1 and 3 promptly lit up. I banged on the call button and showed our no smoking seat stub to the stewardess. "You are not smoking," she explained, "and so this row is not smoking. They are smoking, and so their rows are in the smoking section." Her logic was as faultless as could be. There was absolutely no point in pursuing the matter further.

Indian Airlines served up a vegetarian curry dinner which raised jalapina-like welts on the lips. A lingering kiss of the air-conditioning nozzle would have been wonderful.

Calcutta – pitch black and oppressively steamy. While Gill and Mickey looked after claiming the bags, I engaged in an unreal conversation with the Air India agent and the Indian Airlines supervisor, trying to get them to understand that between them they were responsible for our having missed every connection to Bogdogra, and that without confirmation on tomorrow's flight we would miss our party, and the whole trip would have to be scrubbed. Further, thanks to them, we were absolutely exhausted, and they would have to put us up for the night at their expense. Playing on their sense of compassion, and the fact that I had no intention of moving until I received satisfaction, Air India finally gave me three vouchers for something called "the Oberoi Grand," the only hotel where they were able to get three single rooms. Then ensued a comical game of musical taxis. Our duffle bags were strapped and unstrapped to the roofs of three taxis before someone agreed to take us the 25 kilometers to Calcutta. According to the taxi driver, Air India's vouchers were not always honoured. Late at night, not having any idea where we were going, we headed for town.

"Pen, don't fail me now!" We swerved to avoid people squatting over a stream of their own making; every ledge and windowsill was littered with sleeping bodies; a theatre marquee was 'home' to hundreds, lined up like endless photos of the Jonestown body count; communal rickshaws with 50-foot bamboo sections by the ton were pulled and pushed by three or four human engines; rickshaws were drawn with mechanical steps at this late hour miles from anywhere; an ancient crone tried to resuscitate a motionless body among hundreds of other motionless bodies; sacred cows and rabid

dogs filled the street, and the all-pervading sight and stench of unrelenting, endless, hopeless, massive poverty was everywhere. The entire area smelled like a feculent Augean stable needing the urgent attention of some Indian Hercules. There are simply no words in the English language to convey the battering of the mind and senses encountered in the slums of Calcutta at night.

Countless turns down narrow streets lit only by the foul smudge-pots of the cooking fires of dung cakes, through

a frightful world in which we would be at the mercy of fate if we were ever to be involved in an accident, run over someone or worse, hit a cow. We would disappear without a trace.

Then suddenly, the Oberoi Grand, a tunnelled entrance guarded by a towering turbaned doorman and two armed guards. Up some wide stairs and away from the cruel truth of Calcutta into a different world. The Oberoi Grand is, quite simply, one of the finest hotels in the world. Everything reeks of sandalwood oil; polished marble corridors were thickly carpeted; an oiled teak door was inlaid with massive brass numbers; the furniture was beautiful; and hand-coloured lithographs tastefully framed and not stained with damp recalled the Imperial glories of the days of Kipling. Upstairs the walls were lined with more hand-coloured lithos and engravings of Indian parrots and other birds. Everywhere a sense of calm and timelessness had risen above the petty squabbles of a given age.

It was now well past midnight, but room service brought hot chocolate, toast and jams and soda water with which to brush our teeth. The rooms had no windows, but were clean and safe from the horrors of the world outside. The bathrooms were of polished marble, and the water was hot. The heavy linen sheets were clean and starched, and sleep, after all this time, was blessed.

October 6 – Monday. Complimentary morning paper without any news of the outside world. Then to the Garden Café, across the glassed-in corridor that ran around the 150-foot square palm court, with its pool and gardens, and ubiquitous house crows. It's 7:45 A.M. and the blue sky above this giant atrium is already super-saturated with steamy oppressiveness. Inside, air conditioning, polished brass, crystal chandeliers and more lithographs of colonial times. The staff still padded about in slippers, brandishing feathered dusters. The café serves Bournvita Horlicks, fresh oranges and mangos next to a glassed-in room of budgies that are better fed than the masses in the streets.

In view of the fact that we were meant to arrive in Darjeeling the day before, it seemed appropriate to send a cable to Daku announcing our arrival on today's noon flight. A not-too-cryptic message was composed and given to the telex operator. In the meantime, Gillian and Mickey were arranging for a taxi tour of the city which would deposit us at the airport just before flight time. We were standing at the counter when the telex man came up to us with bad news: "Darjeeling is in the hills, you understand. Inclement weather, sir, cable may not get through. . . ." And he just stood there. I turned to the elegant hostess and said: "I am asking this out of complete ignorance of things Indian. Would a tip help clear up the inclement weather?" "Yes," she smiled, "it probably would." I followed the little man back to a cavernous telex room, crammed to overflowing with papers and boxes, and barely large enough to hold a vintage cable-sending machine with a key board that looked like a carillon. With all the nervousness of a concern pianist, the operator shuffled and stacked papers, adjusted his seat, and almost flipped up his coattails before sitting down to perform. With great ceremony, he cracked his knuckles and faced the keys. The instant he banged the first letter, all the lights in the hotel went out. Our telex never arrived in Darjeeling, and he kept the tip.

Our city tour, with 'an English-speaking driver' who always called Gillian and Mickey, "sir," was awfully hot and sultry. Calcutta by day is overwhelmed by traffic. Rickshaws, endless bazaars, horns blowing, troops of cattle – sacred or profane – bicycles, pedestrians, venerable buses and dump trucks spilling their human cargo out through the windows, commuters on the roofs, beggars, official-looking barristers with furled umbrellas waiting for clients at the law offices, black kites and vultures, goatherds and shepherds grazing their flocks in the largest city park across from the startlingly huge white Victoria Memorial, shimmering above its mirror image in the leaden surface of the reflecting pond. The Memorial is as empty as it is vast. It was built in 1942 as a make-work project, and was never intended to serve a real function. So much of India seems to be – or to need – a make-work project.

As it was a bank holiday, most of the major buildings were closed, and the grounds of those that we could visit were untidy and untended. The lush vegetation seemed poised to reclaim everything that man had introduced. Our tour led down to the edge of the Hoogly which rolled like a malevolent being toward the sea. The waves and currents boiled silently against unseen impediments, causing the surface to erupt in constantly changing patterns of oil slicks. Surrounding each rainbow of filth, the waters ran a flat, completely opaque, yellow-brown. A sidewalk citizen was standing ankle deep to draw his water in a bucket. There was not a hint of his feet, not a trace of the bucket below the surface.

A dirty white freighter lay anchored at the end of a floating pier. Tied up alongside were half a dozen banana-shaped 'bum boats,' their lines the product of millennia of use for which modern technology could find no improvement. A small brown boy stood on the foredeck of his home playing with five pastel-coloured balloons. In the main flood, gigantic buoys bobbed up and down against slime-festooned chains. Small river craft, a thousand years old in their design, plied their way under power supplied by four or five men walking in tandem along the sloping decks, poles mired in the Gangetic wastes. Serpentine prows and lanteen sails, rowers and oars silhouetted against the grey sky.

Back inland water buffalo were lolling in ponds, and whole families of Indians with their belongings in migration from one pocket of hopelessness to another. Naked children splash in the gutters awash with human excrement. Filth, noise and disease permeate everything. Our driver makes sure that no photos can possibly be taken as he lurches around explodingly stuffed street cars heading right for us. The non-vehicular traffic is beyond belief. Rickshaws everywhere. Every scene is a time capsule: barrel makers, sidewalk barbers, coconut vendors, fresh crabs in panniers scuttle against the reed lattice lids suspended swaying from shoulder yokes. And with the time ticking by, there does not seem to be the slightest hope of getting to the airport on time. Then up over a bridge above yards filled with trains that would thrill a railroad buff, and we are on the road to the airport, past rectangular ponds where grassy banks are patrolled by egrets and paddy birds – white winged against brown bodies – and where the waters are shared by dimpling fish, buffalo, human bathers and washers. A slender woman in a beautiful mauve sari disrupts her own reflection in a paddy framed with palms. Scores of school children in matching uniforms head home past endless rows of hovels which breathe the cooking fires' smoke through pores of skin, fur, concrete, metal or cardboard while bodies sleep or slump or squat.

We boarded our flight for Bogdogra in early afternoon, and found that our assigned seats had recently been victimized by three airsick passengers. We sat in the front row along with two truly beautiful children who were returning from hospital in plaster casts. With the countless hordes of maimed and disfigured, how were they chosen to receive medical attention? What would they grow up to be? We pondered these and other matters over a vegetarian lunch served in

House Crow.
Corvus Splendens

a soggy cardboard box. The ever-increasingly fertile land slipped away under us as we headed north. We had hoped for our first view of the Himalayas, but a seething black wall of cloud blocked out everything. We landed at the old-fashioned airport, 400-plus feet above sea level, and 31°C. The bags were loaded onto hand-pulled carts and unceremoniously dumped in a heap in the courtyard under a sign forbidding any picture taking. The bags disappeared one by one into the crowd which in turn dispersed. Finally, we were the only ones left, with our nine pieces of luggage. No one from Mountain Travel or from Daku Norgay's office was waiting for us – only the various kinds of police all had a chance to look through our papers. Yes, one of the officials did remember seeing Daku herself yesterday. No, there was no way of contacting her by phone. Darjeeling was a three hour drive away, and there were no buses. Paras, a most diminutive driver, appeared and offered to drive us to Darjeeling. The bags were bigger than his car. Crammed into the back seat, we headed along the last flat land we were to see for the next three weeks.

Some say that the *real* India lies in the Plains. To the endless horizon paddies were tended by the current generations, repeating a scene unchanged for hundreds, perhaps thousands of years. Silt-laden streams, flowing surprisingly fast, scour away banks they have built up in seasons past. Here and there, a Mediterranean-looking red-tiled village slumbers undramatically under the yellow-blossom shade of mimosa and palm. Paddy birds flap heavily, egrets strike poses in the drainage ditches and buffalo wallow. The highway with no contours with which to conflict is straight as an arrow across the plain. There are no major towns in sight, but the traffic is horrific. Bullock carts with gigantic wooden slab wheels groan along under massive loads of grass, bamboo and people.

Public Carriers – the gaudiest of buses and trucks – are crammed to overflowing, rickshaws number in the hundreds, flocks and herds abound, and saris and furled umbrellas add a colourful touch. Perfect posture is maintained under towering vases. Despite their numbers, these fellow travellers give way to the convoys of army trucks that dominate everything.

And then the plain ends; the hills begin. The road up from Bogdogra to Darjeeling is, from a naturalist's point of view, one of the most interesting in the world. In the space of an hour, you climb almost seven thousand feet, passing through several distinct forest zones on the way, which clothe and protect the very precipitous flanks of these foothills of the Himalayas. The hot, dusty (or soggy) plains are left behind as soon as the road gains altitude, and the vegetation immediately becomes riotous. Huge trees with fluted and sculptured roots buttressing 15 feet up the trunk are linked at their canopies by massive lianas. Giant bamboo, a foot in diameter, segments 18 inches long sprout like so many Cyclopean whiskers. Screw pines and an artist's palette of wild flowers and ferns complete the undergrowth. At about the 4000 foot level, oaks and several species of rhododendrons predominate before succumbing at 6000 feet to a mixed forest of silver firs, magnolias, maples, birch and small bamboo. From there up to the passes and summits as high as 8000 feet, the conifers take over with hemlock, spruce, blue pine, more silver firs, junipers and a dense cover of shrub-like rhododendrons. Across a broad slice of these zones, great cut-leaved Rhapidophora twine about and drape the trees.

Nearer the upper levels, tea plantations or estates replaced the natural growth with their rounded low trees. Young girls, like so many aphids, harvest the tiny leaves which they deposit in their truncated cones of wicker baskets. And all around are thousands of butterflies and birds which the

bouncing car and my own inexperience made impossible to identify. Competing for our attention, however, was a narrow gauge railroad which shared, paralleled, intersected and plagued the road. The toy trains announced their presence with the shrillest of steam whistles, preceded by a plume of white vapour against the belching blackness of the smoke stack.

In one village, the traffic came to a complete halt because the train station was smack in the middle of the road. The Lilliputian engine and blue wagons were a source of fascination and potential commerce for all the villagers, merchants and tourists, including a nattily attired communist Chinese embassy official in blue jacket, trousers and puffy cap, all piped in red. Slung around his neck was a Nikon. This scene would have been unthinkable only a few short years ago.

The enforced wait gave us our first opportunity to study a hill town. Everything was built on levels, with the shops doubling as homes. Most buildings that faced onto the main street (and railroad track) were open to the world, with only an overhanging roof standing between the occupants and the weather. Merchandise was hung from every available peg, and the sense of bustle was evident. The people were beautiful compared to those of the plains, but the poverty was still grinding. At least here, people are closer to the source of food, and the barter system still has a chance to operate.

The train finally shrieked into motion, and the waiting passengers crammed themselves back into the cars, or on the roof if they had to. Small dogs barked, and with tongues flapping out of their mouths, they chased the mechanical toy up the steep incline. By now, we had to buck the traffic that had been building up in the other direction. Trucks far too large for the road careered down upon us, all the more alarming as the weather began to turn decidedly nasty. From the overhanging hairpin turns we could see thick masses of cloud rolling up the valleys, and now the sodden overcast settled down to join everything in swirling mists. The road crossed a local height of land at the village of Kounseng. Here, at almost exactly 7000 feet, the railroad headed down towards fabled Darjeeling. The light was fast fading, and the mists and clouds wrapped the view in total obscurity. Rain had begun to fall, and after three hours in the cramped car we were tired and cold. Welcome to Darjeeling.

Our driver stopped on a switch-back and exchanged news with a handsome sherpa who turned out to be Daku Norgay's brother-in-law and assistant in the travel business that she and her husband operated. Our permits had arrived that very morning! The rest of the group had had a vote and had decided they would wait one more night before leaving without us. And supper would be ready at The Planters' Club Hotel in 45 or so minutes. Daku herself arrived, and wished us a welcome that was friendlier than anything we had experienced down on the plains. We would learn that no person warmer than Daku existed. The taxi drove up a steep hill, and passing in front of some tantalizing shops filled with antiques, stopped in a broad parking area under the cascading carpet of marigolds that blanketed the slope leading up to our hotel.

All of Darjeeling is built on the face of a steep incline, and so virtually every spot affords a fine view – or so the tourist brochures say. At this particular moment, however, all we could see was the monsoon. The city cowered under a wet blanket, with the occasional coloured umbrella bobbing along over unseen feet. Gas lamps and the occasional cooking fire infused the clouds with a halo of light, but basically, everything seemed sombre. Even the hotel – especially the hotel – was damp. The Planters' Club is a long two-storey building with verandahs running the entire length of both floors. Off these balconies the guest rooms open upstairs, with the private and public rooms on the ground level. The bedrooms were reached through individual sitting rooms filled with wicker chairs lined up facing the 'view' through expanses of small window panes. The bedrooms were sparsely furnished with sagging beds arranged around a totally English, totally inadequate fireplace. In the grate several lumps of coal sputtered and smoked ineffectually. From the impossibly high ceilings, bare bulbs hung down on braided cords. Up a step, and into the bathroom with an antique tub easily five and a half feet long, perched on ball and claw feet. The tour was interrupted by the arrival of a small, white-uniformed attendant bearing Darjeeling tea in a pot under a cosy. Slices of toast were cooling in a toast rack. Daku joined us and we talked about the trip. She will be our lead sherpa.

Dinner was in a cavernous converted ballroom so poorly lit that we could not really see what was at the other end. Scattered between us, there was a handful of other guests who sat wondering who and what the long table of westerners was. The group we were to join was already seated when we came in, and they eyed us – we thought, anyway – as we once did the new arrivals at summer camp. Whatever their impressions may have been, there was an overriding sense of delight that we had come. Our three put the total number of trekkers over the magic figure, and we all would be entitled to a reimbursement of $230 from Mountain Travel! We became acquainted over fried fish with limes, gluttonous fricassee of chicken, noodles, potatoes, beans, curry and Black Label (not Carling's) beer in very large bottles. Crème brûlé for dessert and steaming tea rounded out the meal. As the feeling came back to our fingers and toes, we became aware of the rest of the dining room which was cluttered with the blackened trophy horns of gaur, various mountain sheep

and other ungulates sacrificed by bored army officers during the days of the Empire. A huge glass-covered case contained a score of silver cups and awards won by various regiments years ago in sports that can only be guessed at. It could not have been polo; there isn't a level spot in town.

First impression of the group: Bruce Klipinger, our leader, will be strong; the Australian doctors Kendall Frances, Peter and Philippa Currie, Richard Newing and Malcolm Dickson seem rugged and share a twinkle in the eye; a young American, Greg Staple, and the young American photographer, Marion Patterson; and an American couple, recently married, exude very difficult vibrations.

The most fascinating of the bunch is not even a part of it. Ms. Marigold Wisden, secretary of the Planters' Club, breezed in trailing a billow of smoke from her endless cigarettes. An absolute clone of Mrs. White from Bantry, she is the perfect English expatriate who has turned to drink and smoke and locals for diversion and a semblance of sanity. We were to learn later that she had been married nine or ten times. Perhaps none of her husbands, of whatever ethnic background, could stand her twelve Lhasa Apso dogs which followed her, yapping at her heels, everywhere she seemed to go. But for all that, she was a mainstay in the foreign community, and she proved wonderfully kind when the banks were closed.

With bottles of spring water under our arms, we climbed back up to the verandah for a last look at Darjeeling. The rain had let up only momentarily, and the clouds lifted a bit. All we could see was a jumble of cliff-hanging architecture – "the fabulous caprice of unsettled taste." Then into the giant tub with its single faucet providing a private Himalayan torrent and live steam each within five minutes. The tub never filled up, because the hotel water was turned off at

11 P.M. To the sound of temple gongs and ceaseless rain, we finally turned in. The iodine pills would work on the bottled water overnight.

After almost three full days of travel, we were finally here! Tomorrow we spend seven more hours in the cars to Gangtok. But now, sleep, albeit in damp linen.

For centuries, the Arabs had a virtual monopoly on the sea trade with India and China. The goods reached western Europe through the intermediation of the Jews who acted as the commercial bridge that spanned the gulf between Moslem and Christian. The Arab knowledge of winds and currents was as extensive as it was secretive, and under the canopy of this navigational expertise they sheltered a phenomenally successful merchant colony, which, if contemporary figures are to be believed, was wiped out in the massacre of Hangchow in A.D. 875 leaving 26,000 foreigners dead. This put a crimp in the trading patterns for the next several centuries, with commerce withering to sporadic contact through the two great remaining Arab stations of Kalah on the Malay Peninsula and Galle on the southern tip of Ceylon. India and China became, for the West, a closed world enveloped in an ever-thickening blanket of ignorance lavishly embroidered with myth and superstition. In 1498, having circumnavigated Africa, the great Portuguese explorer, Vasco da Gama, was led across the Indian Ocean by an Arab pilot who made use of the favourable and predictable winds that blew in their season. The Arabic word for season was *muasim;* in Portuguese the transliteration was *mançao.* Dutch traders gave their phonetic equivalent as *monssoen.* The monsoon entered our language in the sixteenth century, and entered my room through a leaky window on October 7.

The monsoon, which was meant to have stopped, pounded all night with great rolling claps of thunder and pyrotechnical displays of lightning. Darjeeling averages 123 inches of rain per year, and it seemed as if half of that fell during this one twelve hour period. The monsoon, technically, is not the rain, but rather the wind that carries the rain from the Indian Ocean. From April to early October the southwesterly winds blow against the massive flanks of the Himalayas which forces the air up to levels where it cools and expands. As a result, the rains pour out.

In the late seventeenth and eighteenth centuries, two Englishmen, Edmund Halley (of comet fame) and George Hadley, published scientific treatises which still provide two-thirds of the explanation for the monsoon patterns. Halley in 1686 theorized that differential heating of the oceans and the land masses would cause different air pressures which could only be equalized through winds. Hadley added the explanation that the rotation of the earth and its spherical shape would deflect winds crossing the equator to veer to the right in the Northern Hemisphere and to the left in the Southern – the coriolis effect. We now know that a third factor exists which gives rise to some of the special characteristics of the monsoon. Energy is required to change the state of water into vapour. The energy that is used to effect that change is stored in the molecules of the water vapour as kinetic energy. When the vapour condenses again as rain, the energy is released. An estimated one-sixth of the solar energy that reaches the earth is stored in the vapour that evaporates from the oceans. During the monsoon, this incredibly large reservoir of energy stored in the vapour is released over the land, and is responsible for the awesome power and the duration of the rainy season, as well as influencing the wet and dry spells, known as the active and dormant phases, within the monsoon season itself. Sir Joseph Dalton Hooker, one of the most eminent nineteenth century naturalists, explored this whole area, and

in 1848 he wrote: "Vapours raised from an ocean whose nearest route is more than 400 miles distant are safely transported without the loss of one drop of water to support the rank luxuriance of this far distant region. This and other offices fulfilled, the waste waters are returned by the rivers to the ocean, and again exhaled, exported, recollected and returned!" Hooker was not quite accurate: the monsoon does leak quite a lot along the way, but most of its load is dumped on the southern and middle slopes of the hills.

The next morning we were introduced to what is considered an Indian custom, but really is an English habit that was exported throughout the Empire – morning tea. In a wave of nostalgia that took me back to my family home in Ireland, I sipped the tea and munched the cold toast that had been brought to me at first light. Outside, the fabled view of the Himalayas hid behind the all-enveloping clouds and rain. After breakfast of hot porridge, fried eggs, assorted jams and marmalades and, of course, tea, we repacked our nonessentials into small lockable, rigid cases which we would leave at the hotel for our return. Everything else was stuffed into our duffles, and placed outside on the verandah. An elderly porter, surely not five feet tall, casually picked up three very large bags which must have weighed well over a hundred pounds and carried them – at a trot – down the walkway to the waiting cars. By half past eight our convoy started back down the labyrinthine streets of Darjeeling to the road for Sikkim.

As we broke out over the height of land at Kounseng, we left the clouds, suddenly, breathtakingly, behind. We were in the purest of sunlight, and the vegetation glistened. Skirting the backside of the mountains we had travelled yesterday, we headed up through tea plantations, and then down a corkscrew road through ever-increasing forests of teak trees with

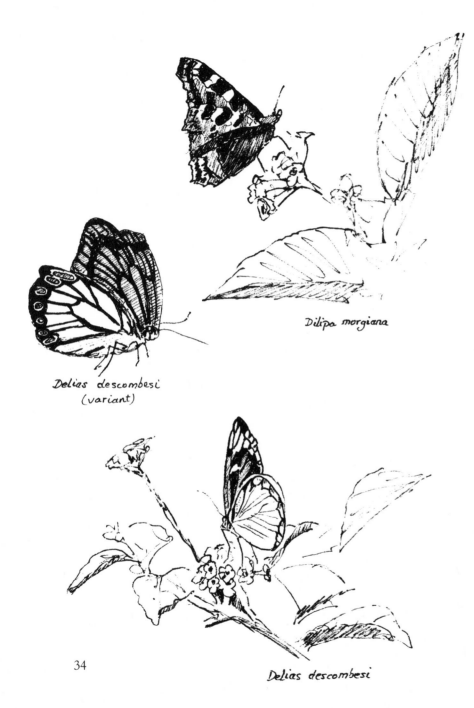

Dilipa morgiana

Delias descombesi
(variant)

Delias descombesi

their giant leaves, shaggy unkempt 'river gums,' (the eucalyptus that had been imported from Australia), bamboo and vines. Richard Newing displayed a profound knowledge of flora, just one of the many hobbies that gave even greater breadth to this wonderful Australian surgeon who specialized in reconstructive surgery. The roadside was flanked with marigolds, cosmos and lilies. Their tubular flowers were easily a foot long. There were unseen birds chattering from the trees, and butterflies as big as birds hovered on iridescent wings. At a scenic roadstop we saw a bright green Indian lorikeet flash by, and a large bug-eyed locust. Down through the trees we could see the Teesta River roil with grey brown silt. Across the river was Sikkim, but hours would pass before we would be able to cross. Through a couple of check points and across a suspension bridge – suspension, because that is what we felt wondering if we would ever make it! It swayed awfully despite the fact that we went one car at a time, and never at more than five miles per hour. Of interest too were the large fruit bats that hung down grotesquely from the transmission wires on which they had been electrocuted. Endless sheets of spider webs festooned everything.

The road became so serpentine that in several spots it actually looped under itself. Nowhere was it more than a car wide, but this did not seem to bother the drivers of the buses that insisted on their right of way. A troop of rhesus monkeys sat vacantly along the side of the road waiting for either a handout or an accident. Mountain sparrows and mynahs were the birds most in evidence.

By midday we arrived at the Zangdogpalriphodang monastery, outside of Kalimpong. Our tour was perfunctory, and the impression fades immediately into an overall mosaic of hideous faces, layered embellishments, garish colours, dragons and a lama who tried to sell us some of the temple's treasures from under the folds of his robe. We would see other and better temples later. For now, lunch was of prime interest.

The sun was beautifully warm in Kalimpong. The town was a riot of colourful saris, fruit stands, piles of apples under an umbrella, a salesman (with his Himalayan cat) who sold loofahs, brooms, melons and tobacco, brilliantly coloured laundry waving from the decayed arch of a house of faded grandeur. But above all, Kalimpong means butterflies. Next to the Tibetan Refugee Centre where we had our picnic lunch there was a long bank of pink and yellow flowers. They swarmed with stunningly beautiful butterflies. The *Delias descombesi* showed bright yellow on the under lower wing, with a tear drop of crimson, then the black and white reticulations of the upper wing. Seen from above, everything was snowy white. The *Dilipa morgiana* was a puzzle of golden oranges and browns.

A local football match had swelled the town to festive capacity. The free-wheeling architecture, the stern rustic-gothic Church of England, the sights and sounds and smells – the silversmith blowing, the shoemakers with their salvaged rubber tires for repairs, the laughing young schoolgirls in their uniforms – nothing could seem more exciting and yet more peaceful. Only eight kilometers away, Indian and Chinese armies have clashed.

After lunch we descended by twisted roads through the lush forest, with waterfalls over or on the roadbed, past jungle villages in which the thatched longhouses looked more Javanese than Indian, down through a thousand shades of green to the valley floor where the Teesta and the Ranggit compete with the Colorado for silent walls of silken water that dissolve in thundering foam over hidden rocks. Through no less than three more check points, across another suspension bridge

and, under a spreading mimosa tree, into the market town of Rangpo, our first entrance to Sikkim. Then, just as we had come spiralling down, so now we spiralled up a handmade road past hand painted signs on blind corners ("Did you leave the children smilling at home?" 'Smilling' wasn't a mistake; we saw it everywhere. It was policy!); up through rice paddies terraced over generations, up a vertical mile to Gangtok, a thrilling layered city, a true Shangri-La as the lights twinkled into being.

It was impossible to guess the population of the former nation's capital. It was also impossible to define where the city began and ended. Gangtok means "top of the hill," and, straddling as it does a ridge between two vast valleys, the name is appropriate. But the city proper, concentrated in parallel lines along the uppermost reaches of the valley walls, thins out as it descends, blending imperceptibly with the houses and farms that steal valued space from the countless terraces stepping away far below to the silent grey ribbon of siltwater which scours the jumbled rocks of the valley floor several thousand feet down. A distinction between the city and its hinterland is arbitrary.

Exactly who constitutes the population also requires an arbitrary definition. As if leading to a disorganized ant hill, the twisting road up to the city carried endless convoys of army trucks in both directions, simultaneously relieving and reinforcing the troops that are stationed in the mountain fastness of the Chinese frontier not many miles away. The olive drab, stern looking Sikhs with their nattily bound turbans, the huge drain on the public exchequer represented by these men and material – it all seemed somewhat anachronistic. It would take little to blast the roads into oblivion; they had a habit of falling under their own weight. The hills were too precipitous for mass troop movements, and the altitude would surely cut down on a man's will to fight and on his ability to function. But the troops were moving, and the contrast with the local population was startling. Invariably, the army personnel were healthier, better housed and certainly better fed. Gangtok was filled with troops. Should they be counted among the population?

Most of the traffic was not, however, vehicular. Tight little knots of male and female labourers impinged on the limited roadway as they hammered and chipped at the rocks that would be converted into roadbed. The workmen of all ages sat with their black umbrellas tightly furled, or squatted in bare feet, silently and impassively watching as streams of merchants trudged by. Peasants were transformed into quivering stacks of branches and leaves from which two feet emerged. Clusters of school girls in various uniforms would smile and wave before the youngsters would suddenly disappear over the side of the road into apparent oblivion to their farm homes below. The young boys were much more taciturn. There were people everywhere, climbing or descending depending on their mission.

A huge billboard sponsored by the state oil monopoly urged everyone to conserve gas, or, it warned ominously, the last drop would drip in another 20 years. It seemed a bit incongruous, exhorting these shoeless peasants to conserve something that meant so little to their daily lives. Most would never set foot in a motorized vehicle, and those that would would almost certainly cram themselves in "Public Carriers," privately owned dilapidated open trucks, the kind horrible headlines are made of. The trucks were gaudy to a fault, so totally exaggerated in design that they could truthfully be called 'taste-free.' The windows of the cab were inevitably festooned with every conceivable bangle designed to distract at best and obscure at worst, the driver's vision. The front licence plate on one cab wished everyone "Good Luck!", but a mangled man's shoe, impaled on the corner, indicated that not everyone had been blessed. There were buses, too, and they were frighteningly overloaded with parts of human anatomy protruding from every window. Clouds of pitch black slimy exhaust enveloped everything as the under-powered engines screamed in protest against the laws of gravity. With all these people coming and going, who could say what the population might be? Someone assured us that Gangtok was "bigger than Darjeeling," but this can almost certainly be discounted as a chauvinistic boast. In 1970, the population was officially estimated at 12,000; by 1980 it was probably twice that. In Sikkim – in all India – precision is not easy, nor is it, as someone else pointed out, necessary. The impression that lingered was one of a city with too many people for its size.

The sun set behind the purpling hills and bathed Kangchenjunga in mauve. Mickey and Gillian were fast asleep when we finally stopped in front of the Tashi Delek, our excellent hotel. In the crowded main square outside, horns blared and humans seethed in countless numbers. Rising above such pettiness was the totally tranquil statue of Gandhi, draped in the white cotton scarves which were also draped around our necks as "honoured guests" by the hotel keeper as we came in. The entrance to the hotel was a narrow door under an elaborate pagoda-type arch which led to a long passage at the end of which was a reception room fronted in turn by a flowered patio overlooking the city and the hills beyond. The actual hotel occupied the nine floors below. Like almost everything else in Gangtok, the Tashi Delek was built on the side of a steep hill.

The rooms were tasteful, simple and spotless. We quickly unpacked, ordered bottled water and reconvened upstairs

for tea with Daku. She has been to the Explorers Club in New York, has travelled with Lars Eric Lindblad to the Antarctic, knows Roger and Jinny Peterson, Sir Peter and Philippa Scott, and fondly remembers our dear friend Eric Shipton. Her son had applied to Dartmouth for September 1981. Never has there been a more pleasant tea!

There was still enough light for some sightseeing. There were flowers everywhere – blue, white, red and rose cosmos, wild trumpet lilies, hibiscus of many shades, bougainvillea and mimosa. Clouds of tiny yellow butterflies exploded from blossoms and from cut stone walls. On first impression, Gangtok easily surpasses Darjeeling in cleanliness and pride, even beauty; but then again, we could not possibly have seen Darjeeling in worse conditions. We'll reserve judgment until later.

There were no street lights, but there were lamps in the stalls that were still open. We watched with interest as a vendor, with great flourish, stripped the veins from a fresh, waxy-looking leaf of the Betel-pepper tree (Piper betal) before smearing a combination of the fruits of the Betel-nut palm (Areca catechu) with lime plus assorted spices ladled from silver pots of glorious symmetry. This is the chewing gum of the East, and in the name of sparkling white teeth and dark gums, everyone indulges in the habit. Unfortunately, betel stimulates a tremendous flow of saliva, and the sidewalks are dripping in blood red splats of expectorations. As uncouth as it seems, even the finest people participate. Dr. Dick insisted that the whole muck is addictive and quite probably carcinogenic.

Chinese food for dinner, and more white scarves. Endless tea, and great conviviality as the various members of the group exchanged their stories and impressions of the long day's drive. It is fascinating to note how different eyes see very different things. And yet, we all passed by the same route.

After dinner, we all went out onto the roof terrace, and were treated to the most brilliant display the skies can offer. The Milky Way was resplendent, and stars which would have been invisible to the naked eye in our smog-ridden cities shone clearly. Every few minutes, a meteorite scratched the heavens.

The bathrooms were strange. There was no subdivision for the shower. The whole thing is a shower. But the water was hot, the beds were clean and dry, and the morning would come all too soon. We would be called for morning tea at 5 A.M., and then go out onto the terrace to watch the sun come up on K3, Kangchenjunga, at 28,130 feet the third highest mountain in the world, and, we were told, right on our doorstep!

The house boy rapped on the door at 5 A.M. with a steaming pot of tea and a rack of cold toast. Outside, the light was still grey in the pre-dawn. By 5:15 we had gathered on the patio to wait for one of the most spectacular sunrises I've ever experienced. At 5:30 the sun rose directly behind our backs, and, directly in front of us, the third highest mountain on earth, Kangchenjunga, emerged from the night and assumed a thousand cloaks of increasingly brilliant hues. The pre-dawn turned the mountain and its sister peaks to a flat wall of mother-of-pearl in which the opalescence intensified with an almost pregnant air. Then suddenly the rays of the new sun bathed the very summit in liquid gold which cascaded down the flanks, adding not only colour but also contrast. The direct sun emphasized the folded, jagged cliffs, crevasses, outcroppings, sculptured and rounded glacial pockets, cirques and arrets, and boldly etched the contradictions of snow and massive rock. This incredible scene towered above the valley at our feet, a valley still absolutely in the dark. As each moment slipped by, the light changed, patterns elusively dissolved into new ones. By 6 A.M. the mountain had assumed its full

The Lall Market
Gangtok, Sikkim.
Oct. 1980, from
Michey's Window.

-45-

40

role of command over its kingdom, while the Lal Market unshuttered and the worthy citizens of Gangtok began another day.

To them, it was old hat. Their great mountain had given them this virtuoso performance since the beginning of time. From earliest years they had been taught that the name literally meant "The House of the Five Treasures," represented by the five soaring peaks that make up the massif. The treasures are the gold that is lacquered on them by the rising and setting sun, the silver from the sparkling mantle of renewed snow, and the jewels from the sacred scriptures that contain the teachings of the Gods and the Enlightened Reincarnates who dwell in the mountain fastness. And they have long since ceased to question the fact that this is the ancestral home of the Yeti, or Abominable Snowman.

I put away the camera, and Dick put away his box of water colours, and, with more than an hour before breakfast, we climbed down the ladder-like steps to the Lal Market. Set out in orderly rows, the corrugated tin roof sheds formed an almost military compound, but the organization that this would imply disappeared with the opening of each individual stall. There were bags of garlic buds, herbs and spices, mounds of yellow turmeric, neat piles of tomatoes, apples, oranges – bright green – and frighteningly long and suggestive squashes. Hand woven fabrics in bolts and carpets teetered, chickens and ducks complained through the lovely lattice patterns of their prison baskets, or lost their footing as they were jostled, captive on the back of their merchants in their esthetically and functionally beautiful final carrying cases. A foot here, a tail there, and a beak alternately filled and emptied the spaces between the splits of bamboo.

And everywhere were the children. Tiny twins in matching sweaters striding purposefully hand in hand to whatever destination held urgency for five-year-olds. Infants bulged

Another "suspension" bridge!

from shawls on their sisters' or perhaps mothers' backs, while others suckled contentedly. Intent men squatted by their wares, or stood in tight groups discussing the matters of the day. Porters balanced towering loads of every description as the primitive commerce of the mountains came to life. More accurately, the commerce came together. Many of the farmers had been walking most of the night up the winding road from the valley floor 5000 feet below. Goats and dogs nonchalantly investigated every nook and cranny that might hold food, and men, women and children of all ages availed themselves of the public facilities at the market's edge. The unmistakable stench of humanity stripped the scene of some of its romance.

The shops in the upper town took down their louvered fronts long after the market had opened. Off the main square there were purveyors of everything from shortwave radios and galvanized tin water jugs to elaborate silver filigree boxes encrusted with rough cut semi-precious stones. I bought one, and a red coral necklace to put in it. Then back to the Tashi Delek for breakfast.

At 9 A.M. we squeezed back into our cars and struggled down through the horn-blaring traffic to the leaping river below the city, across a suspension bridge, through clouds of glorious butterflies, intersecting the measured contours of the countless rice paddies, and back up the other side of the valley to the Rumtek Monastery, 23 kilometers and two hours away from Gangtok. The brightly coloured and incredibly ornate four-tiered structure is built in the traditional style of a lamasery of Tibet. Inside, the seven silver bowls of melted butter gave off flickering light beneath the brooding statue of Buddha and all around were the hundreds of other deities in varying poses and grotesqueries that afflict this art form. Filtering through the walls were the moaning,

chanting, repetitive callings of the novice monks who were learning their mantras. We found them on an upper balcony, kneeling towards the wall, swaying back and forth, bending from the waist in a hypnotic trance from which they emerged totally and instantly as soon as they were given the permission to revert to being boys. They then clustered around, fascinated especially by the binoculars and cameras. Their cropped hair and the dark carmine robes set them apart from the normal.

The word in Sikkimese for a monastery is "gompa" which means "a solitary place." Rumtek is perched near the top of the hill diagonally across from Gangtok, with a commanding view of the ranges of hills that lead ultimately to the Himalayas themselves. As the terraces step up the hills and the population begins to implode on the capital city, this particular gompa becomes less and less solitary. The encroaching outside world with its temptations is still kept at bay by the walled courtyard in which the monastery is placed. Some temptations have crept in; one of the lamas offered to sell us some more temple treasures. On the grassy hill outside the compound, tall bamboo poles swayed under the pious tug of Tibetan prayer flags that issued their message through the eternal winds. Marion, meanwhile, gave all the cylindrical prayer wheels a spin for good measure; Daku talked with the lamas; Philippa recorded everything she could on the cassette; and the others bargained for antiques in the little shop down the road. Malcolm, who had suffered through a night of the runs, was seated heavily on a mileage post. "Is that rock doing the job?" Kendall asked to the glee of everyone else. The lightness was a great relief. There is something too unchanging, too alien about the religion and the architecture. Or perhaps we are just too evolved to understand. Nevertheless, I came away with a reinforced personal feeling that there was something basically incomplete with the world espoused by the example of a Buddhist gompa.

Back into the cars for a long, hot ride back up to Gangtok and the hotel for an endless Indian lunch. The afternoon would be spent sightseeing at the royal compound which straddles the crest of the hill on which the city sprawls. Up through an elaborate gate and past bored military personnel on guard to make sure that the ex-king did not escape from his house arrest. We walked around the cool grounds, watched some children playing soccer on the tended grass, two youngsters playing acrobatic ping-pong in the bright yellow open pavilion, and did a quick tour of the royal monastery which exuded a sameness that would deaden our desire for "temple-bashing." The palace itself was a very modest effort for a royal residence. Its peaked bays and lack of flamboyance would have let it pass unnoticed in many of our own suburbs. Inside, the ex-king sulks away his time, feeling, perhaps with justification, that fate has not been too kind to him. Depending on which side of the fence you sit, his country either voted democratically to become India's twenty-second state, or the elections were rigged. His claim to the throne was somewhat tenuous to begin with; the crowning of the first king at Yuksam is either legend or fact, depending on the mists that swirl throughout the history of the mountain kingdoms. In any event, when he gave up hope, Hope gave up the king. Ironically, I was at the Athens Hilton in the mid-1960s when the then-king and his new wife, Hope, were celebrating their marriage, and watched them exchanging lingering glances at the next table.

The friendliness of the people was exceeded by that of a puppy that kept leaping up on Mickey's leg to give her a lick. Gentle push came to not-so-gentle shove, but he persisted. It was only then that we realized that the object of his interest

White-Eye
Zosterops palpebrosa

LARGE PIED WAGTAIL

Motacilla maderaspatensis

43

Lammergeier
Gypaetus barbatus

was not Mickey, but rather something on Mickey's leg, namely blood! Rolling up her pant leg, Mickey discovered the first leech bite of the trip. One of those odious little creatures had inched its way up her sock and injected some local anaesthetic and some anti-coagulant before settling down to a feast. By the time the bite had been found, the leech was long gone, sated for at least another two or three weeks before it would feed again.

We walked back down the winding roads through the upper city to the main square. Smiling children enthusiastically practised their English on us with endearing calls of "I love you," "That's very nice," and "Good Morning!" even though it was now late in the afternoon.

On the way back to the hotel we passed a stand of tall bamboo from which wafted down a lovely song. The exact entry in my diary points out the excitement and anguish of a birdwatcher who has no idea what he's watching: "Saw beautiful yellow-throated yellow-vented vireo-like or large warbler-like bird with a beautiful song – so far no luck in identifying it. Yellow-vented bulbul?" It turned out to be the very common, but very pleasing, white eye *(Zosterops palpebrosa)*. Earlier in the day we had seen several large pied wagtails by the stream.

But by far the most exciting addition to my life list was the Lammergeier. We were driving along a particularly precipitous stretch of road, skirting the terraces that stepped away below towards the valley floor several thousand feet down. Suddenly, a huge bird on whistling wings glided along an unseen contour of the valley walls *below* us. It is from the character in which it is best known to the inhabitants of the German Alps, as the spoiler of the fold, that this bird received its title, the Lammergeier, or "the lamb vulture." It has been accused of carrying off little children, but even with its 10 or 11-foot wingspan, this would seem unlikely. Lammergeier-watching is not, however, without danger for someone like myself, whose hair has euphemistically, thinned considerably. Pliny, in the first century A.D., described how these giants would drop turtles onto rocks below to break open their shells. According to him, Aeschylus was supposed to have been killed when a Lammergeier dropped a turtle on his bald head which he mistook for a rock! Just as he passed under our view, the orange tinge on the throat and chest were visible, as were the black floppy bristles projecting from the base of the lower mandible from which it takes its other name, the Bearded Vulture.

Ornithologically, not a bad day at all. A terribly boring visit to the Institute of Tibetology produced a vivid lime green triangular bug that spat when it was turned on its back. Countless spiders and butterflies rounded out the wildlife.

While we were sliding around the Institute in our stocking feet seeing the butt ends of countless slabs of manuscripts – but not being able to look at the manuscripts – we could have been visiting the orchid sanctuary immediately below which represents most of the more than 600 varieties of orchids found in the country.

Waiting for our Sikkimese dinner to start, I wandered out onto the roof patio and discovered a stupendous bright green katydid perfectly disguised a leaf. As it was clinging vertically to the window pane exactly at eye level, it was a very simple matter to copy its outline, bottom and side view, directly onto the pages of my diary. A group of French tourists arrived noisily, and with the one exception of a woman who had spent some time in Canada, the only interest they evinced for the bug was exaggerated horror. What will the eyes of such people show them of Sikkim!

Our native dinner started with a giant bamboo segment

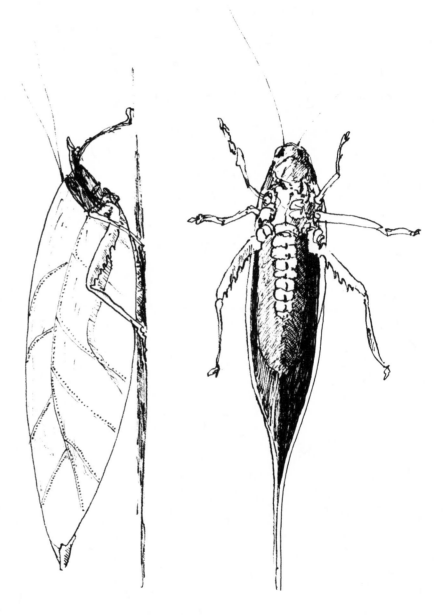

Giant leaf locust

45

full of *tomba*, a warm brew of hot water that percolated down through fermented millet and grains to be sucked very slowly – lest you get a mouthful of grain – through tall straws also made of bamboo shoots. The drink tasted like saki, and as the host kept on adding hot water, and we kept on drinking, it became increasingly obvious that we were in big trouble. Not to worry, we had been told, as the brew was only a week old. In the mountains they let it ferment for months.

The menu was very gluttonous flat noodle soup; side dishes of *mo-mo*, very gluttonous half-moon dumplings with a chewy covering that looked like bite-impressions at the dentist in wax, which were stuffed with spiced chopped meat and dipped into several fire-like sauces. Then fried rice with chicken bits, and chicken with gluttonous sauce with a hint of rose water. The chickens were remarkably scrawny. Roast pork was served with slices of cucumber three and a half inches in diameter, fried fish, mandarine sections and a tumbler of Sikkimese brandy. The folk dancing that had been rumoured for 6:30 was now three hours late. This, and the *tomba*, were good excuses to get the bags packed, have a last shower and a decent night's sleep. A head-clearing stroll on the patio confirmed that the stars were as spectacular as ever. The mountain gods even supplied a fiery shower of meteorites.

October 9 – Thursday. "A decent night's sleep!!!" Gangtok and I awoke at 4 A.M. when someone transferred ownership of his tin can collection to his neighbour living at the bottom of the long flight of steps passing right beside my window down to the market. Some family shared the smoke of their dung cooking fire right through my open window. At 4:30 the compressor started to pump water to the roof. The house boy finally brought morning tea at 6:30. I took my cup to the end of the hall, and watched the mountains emerge to meet the day, but this time they were all pearl grey under the

advancing rows of total cloud cover. By 7:45 the sun had begun to burn the clouds off, and a marvellous day announced itself. I jogged to the general store for postcards, but there was only one of Sikkim – a poinsettia plant. All the others showed various out of focus views of India. Maybe there is a real market here for decent cards, but then again, with only a handful of tourists, maybe there isn't. The exercise was hypothetical in any case, because there wasn't a stamp to be had in Gangtok. The one card that I did leave with the concierge arrived in Canada eight weeks later.

As I jogged back to the hotel, the pan dealers were very active, and so, therefore, were the saliva glands of their customers. As I emerged from behind a parked truck I was just missed by a betel spitter. I took a picture of the proof on the pavement. I also unsuccessfully bargained for a pair of very simple solid gold torques which, as it turned out later, were at least twice the price of similar treasures in Darjeeling.

After breakfast we jammed into the waiting cars for the all day trip to Pemayangtse, the starting point of the actual trek. We retraced our steps down to the Teesta, and started up a new trail that would have been acceptable to most private driveway owners. What the road lacked in width and comfort, it more than made up for in sheer beauty. Sheer, because the surface was carved out of the faces of towering cliffs. This being the tail end of the monsoon season, the outpouring of the clouds was transformed into hundreds, perhaps thousands, of waterfalls springing from the jungle high above, free-falling to be re-absorbed by unseen courses in the jungle below. We came through one particular fall before Gillian could close the car window; it was like driving through a car wash.

The scenery, the terracing, the lushness and the endless shades of green were beyond relief. At about 8000 feet we crossed a pass into a valley in which the slopes faced the opposite direction. The southern exposure of the mountains is noticeably different from the hills facing north. The former mountains are lush, being invigorated by the monsoon, the latter being more bleak, and at altitude, we would learn, even barren.

We stopped for a box lunch at an army basketball court, drank heavily of the breathtaking view, marked the inch-by-inch progress of a leech, felt badly for Mickey who managed to pick up two more leech bites, and photographed a long black-spotted and banded orange beetle.

Projecting from its head were two antennae more than two and a half inches long. There are more than 20,000 known species of the *Cerambycidae*, of which this was one. Probably hundreds more await scientific description. To the layman,

Black spotted orange longicorne beetle

they are all lumped together as the longicorns or long-horned beetles. The antennae are used, as they are by most insects, as smell receptors which the males employ especially during the mating season to pick up the scent of the females. These beautiful beetles play an important role in the recycling of the forest. During their larval stage they are prodigious wood-borers, living on (and speeding up the process of) rotting wood for as long as three years. After emerging as adults, the longicorns feed on flowers and pollen.

This was my first longicorn, and although I am not "bitten" by insects as I am by birds, I nevertheless felt a thrill of discovery. In 1856, the great naturalist, Alfred Wallace Russel, the co-propounder with Darwin of the Theory of Evolution, collected during a single two-week period more than 300 species of longhorns in Sarawak, more than nine-tenths of which were new to science. Of the many thousands of species of insects he is credited with discovering, he felt the longicorns were the "most numerous and interesting group" of beetles. For him, a drawer full of longicorns was the ultimate expression of tropical luxuriance.

The road deteriorated in spots to basic impassability. Every few hundred yards there would be another washout or landslide. "Sinking Road Area" signs made it even more reassuring as we crept along the edge of 500 or 1000 foot drops immediately beside the car. Signs exhorting us to beware of falling rocks seemed somewhat insignificant when the rocks in question were considerably larger than our car. Road gangs made up of equal numbers of men and women chipped away at the boulders, and manually plugged gaping holes in the intermittently paved surface. It was easier to concentrate on the shafts of sunlight that contended with patches of cloud to highlight first one then another rice paddy, or eruption of jungle, or to transform a slender waterfall into a cascade of

THATCHED HUT
AT FOURTEEN MILES
ON THE YOKSAM ROAD

jewels. Here and there, thatched dwellings and isolated villages were betrayed by plumes of blue-grey smoke.

Man had obviously transformed much – most – of the landscape in the lower slopes of the valleys. The terracing was vast, and startling like that which another mountain people in the Andes had created. Here and there were extensive stands of trees, but the prevalence of bamboo was proof of man's interference with the native vegetation. A mature rain forest is incompatible with man's greed. Above a certain line the forest was, however, totally in possession of the slopes. This was one of the last great mature forests in the Himalayas. Once it covered Nepal's Arun Valley, that country's equivalent to Sikkim's Teesta Valley, but an unbridled population explosion coupled with the retention of the old ways has spelled doom for the forests that have been felled for firewood. Erosion has denuded entire valley walls, and even the terracing has slumped into oblivion with catastrophic speed. An ecological disaster is in the making in these same mountains, but no one in an official capacity seems to heed the words of François René de Chateaubriand who, in the 1840s, astutely remarked: "Forests precede peoples and nations; deserts succeed them."

We had been climbing steadily for hours, but we were still very much hemmed in by the steepness of the surrounding hills. Every now and then, a vista back down the valley would open up, with the spurs of the various ranges interlocking or overlapping like cards being shuffled in a pack. But nowhere could we see the giant snow-capped peaks that we knew loomed above. It was frustrating in a sense, but the very fact that we were still denied our first close-ups heightened the sense of anticipation.

The huts and farms were a total surprise. In their form and materials, they looked as if they should have been among the rice fields and jungles of Sumatra, Java or Bali, Thailand or Cambodia. Typically, they had no chimney, the eternal smoke seeping out at either end of the main room through triangular vents that sloped down from, and at right angles to, the pitch of the central roof line. The roofing material was made up of palm fronds lashed together with bamboo, the walls of similar construction. In the more solid buildings, the whole was perched on a foundation of stone covered in white stucco. As old as humanity, the design served the people well, but today, the same design is translated in the more opulent areas into corrugated tin. As Louis Sullivan, the American architect once said, "form follows function," but he might have added that materials follow fads. Tin is more socially desirable than thatch; it is also very unhealthy. There is a serious disease in ventilation which adversely affects the health of the dwellers during the hot season. Status is more important than health.

The most memorable part of the trip that day, however, were the birds. Few are the joys of birding that exceed those of seeing your first members of a brand new species. A dozen such thrills were added to our life list on the road from Gangtok to Pemayangtse. First there was a scarlet minivet, the male in brilliant orange and black, the female with the orange replaced by yellow. A verditer flycatcher flashed by in brilliant blue-green, and the Indian roller (or jay) was electric blue. In the valley floor, white-capped river chats flicked among the rounded boulders. There were whistling thrushes, and a wonderful pair of the dark Himalayan representatives of the peregrine falcon. Himalayan tree pies were very common, dragging their long tails from one tree top to another.

But the two most fantastic birds were the large racket-tailed drongo *(Dicrurus paradiseus)* and Mrs. Gould's sunbird *(Aethopyga gouldiae)*.

Trailing the two 'rackets' from the tips of the two outer tail feathers, the drongo looked at first like a normal black

Flamed or Scarlet
Minivet
(Pericrocotus flammeus)

MRS. GOULD'S SUNBIRD
Æthopyga gouldiae

bird being escorted by two bobbing tiny companions. This was one of the birds I had wanted to see the most, thanks in large measure to the descriptions in Terry Shortt's *Not as the Crow Flies*. (After returning to Canada, I went to visit Peter Buerschaper who had replaced Terry as the head of the art department at the Royal Ontario Museum. On his desk was a stuffed racket-tailed drongo which he had salvaged from behind a display case during the renovations at the R.O.M. It was the very bird that Terry had collected during his famous trip to the Himalayas, and no one seemed to have recognized it. Mysteriously, the bird now resides in my library.)

In total contrast to the black drongo was the glorious gem of the sunbird. The New World boasts of its hummingbirds, and the Old World in Africa and Asia counters with a family of small, scimitar-beaked jewels whose colours in the clear air fairly explode. Mrs. Gould's sunbird is one of several species of yellow-rumped members of this family found throughout the lower altitudes in the Himalayan foothills. The two long tail feathers are a rich metallic blue with shimmering purple reflections. The head, ear coverts and throat, and a spot on each side of the chest near the shoulders, are deep sanguineous red; the rump and the under surface are a bright yellow with the belly having a few red dashes. The overall impression, however, is a blinding flash of red as the bird, with tremendous speed, flies up to and occasionally hovers before tubular flowers, or draws nectar from the drooping tongue of a large hibiscus blossom.

The bird was named by Vigors, *Nectarinia gouldiae* in honour of the immensely talented wife of John Gould, the great impressario of mammoth bird books in England during the mid-to-late nineteenth century. Based on her husband's sketches and layouts, Elizabeth Gould worked up the drawings into their final form on stone, from which they were lithographed and hand-coloured. The first book on which John and Elizabeth Gould collaborated was *A Century of Birds of the Himalayas* published in two sumptuous folio volumes in 1832. With its 80 plates, *Century* seemed a contradiction. Actually, 100 different figures, including males and females, were given, but two of the male birds – including Mrs. Gould's sunbird – were shown in two positions, making the total number of specimens exactly 100, hence *Century*. This is one of the rarest of the great bird books and the quest of every serious collector. Someday, perhaps . . .

We arrived at Pemayangtse after having descended first from 8000 feet to 1000 feet before twisting back up to the delightful hostel at 6800 feet. Functional to a fault on the outside, and sparsely furnished on the inside, the Pemayangtse Tourist Lodge nevertheless was clean, had hot water, and beautifully oiled wooden doors with massive locks, bolts and keys straight out of Mme. Tussaud's Wax Works Chamber of Horrors. What made the lodge so incredible was the site: perched on the crest of a hill, it commanded a 360 degree view of the valleys branching off to the hills, row after row, to the clouds and to the falling night that finally blended earth and air into a gathering jungle.

There was just enough light left before dinner for us to walk over to the monastery, the second oldest in Sikkim, and one of the most holy, in fact the head, of all the monasteries belonging to the Nyingmapa sect. The light faded too fast, and the electric bulbs were too weak – the visit was basically a waste of time. The only thing of interest was a huge intricately carved model of a monastery – or perhaps a whole village. It was too dark to tell. Impressive, certainly, but is it art!

We walked around the grounds of the lodge amid flocks of Himalayan goldfinches, mountain pies, and assorted species of bulbuls in the mixed forests. We also found our first wild

LARGE RACKET-TAILED DRONGO
Dicrurus paradiseus

51

orchid blooming – a lilac trumpet with a yellow mouth striped with interrupted orange and brown.

Waiting for supper, we found that the only literature in the lodge consisted of back issues of a Russo-Indian friendship magazine which were filled with absolute garbage. Worst of all was the special issue devoted to the Moscow Olympics, with endless rhetoric against the U.S.-led boycott. Sports and politics must not mix, say the Russians, who then spend pages in glorifying Moscow as the headquarters of world socialism, the socialist way of life, and the prowess of Russian athletes whose performances are living proof of superiority. Jesse Owens, where are you?

Gillian had begun feeling quite green and missed supper as well as Bruce's detailed introduction to the do's and don'ts for the trek which was to start early the next morning. He outlined some of the symptoms of mountain sickness; reminded us that out of courtesy for local beliefs we must always pass temples and chortons (piled stones or small temples) on the left; never to use open fires or candles in our tents; make all complaints only to our sirdar or to Bruce himself; always make sure that we walked bracketed between the lead and the tail sherpa; and above all, to drink, drink, drink more than we could possibly believe we would need.

I went with Dick and Kendall to their room to sketch a fine selection of moths while all the Australian doctors unconcernedly discussed Gillian's sickness, happily disagreeing about the advisability of Lomotil or other corks. In any event, her fever was brought down, and the runs finally subsided by morning. Mickey, in the meantime, had gone to bed feeling less than perfect, and awoke feeling quite miserable. The trek was off to a good start, and the thought really crossed my mind: "What in the world am I doing here?" My musings, however, were interrupted when I fished a magnificent moth out of the toilet.

52

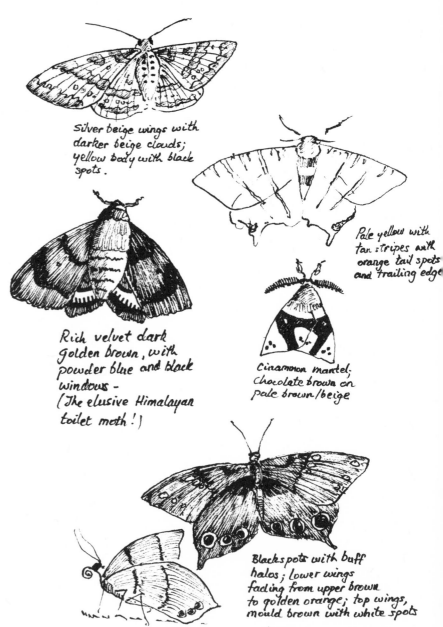

Silver beige wings with darker beige clouds; yellow body with black spots.

Pale yellow with tan stripes with orange tail spots and trailing edge

Rich velvet dark golden brown, with powder blue and black windows –
(The elusive Himalayan toilet moth!)

Cinnamon mantel; chocolate brown on pale brown/beige

Black spots with buff halos; lower wings fading from upper brown to golden orange; top wings, mould brown with white spots

under-wings: mushroom brown with chestnut stripes

one of the Satyridae, but which one?

October 10 – Wake-up tea was brought to the room at 5:30 A.M. Outside the entire 360 degrees was ablaze as the far mountains towered above us in the spectacular sunrise. Below, the valleys lay submerged under a thick blanket of cloud. The surrounding woods were filled with wonderful birds. A male and female chestnut-bellied rock thrush sang from a branch nearby. Minivets, tree pies, goldfinches and a roller showed themselves, but hundreds of others sang from their verdant hiding places, and there was no time to outwait

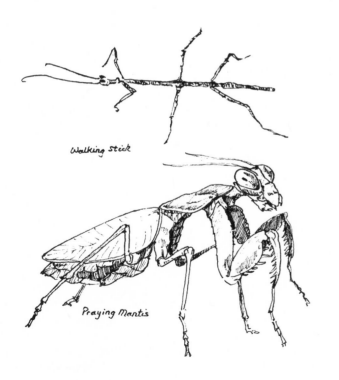

Walking Stick

Praying Mantis

them. And, apart from a walking stick, nothing cooperated long enough for a detailed field sketch. I'm totally frustrated.

At precisely 8:15 A.M. we left the tourist lodge and headed off down the paved road in brilliant sun, to the accompaniment of a thousand avian wishes. So this is trekking! Swinging along in tropical clothes, chatting and laughing under a warming sun. All that was missing were the pith helmets – Gill supplied the English accent. Even the 20-pound packs seemed as nothing. Not 25 meters into the trip, Bruce and the others turned abruptly to the right, over the edge of the road, and straight down into thick jungle over a mica-dusted trail. The buzz of cicadas was a constant ambient noise, on which intruded the occasional flocks of hysterical laughing thrushes. Electric-blue verditer flycatchers sprang from perches for unwary bugs; long coils of lianas drooped from the larger trees; ferns and mosses and countless birds all kept us captivated. We rested briefly at a small clearing beside an impressive stand of giant bamboo *(Dendrocalamus giganteus)* in which lofty culms moaned as they rubbed together. Each segment exceeded 18 inches, and the cross-section was easily a foot. It was here that we found just how numerous the leeches were. They were everywhere. You would stop in an open exposed spot and watch half a dozen suddenly start inch-worming towards you. Mickey seemed very susceptible.

Past isolated farm houses of classic thatch design, past groups of uniformed and smiling lovely school girls, standing barefoot in ideal leech terrain. And we passed chortons on our left, as a sign of respect.

The trail finally focused on a narrow, steeply inclined ridge from which the land on either side sloped away more abruptly than we cared to contemplate to the river. The course carved a horseshoe around the spur ahead, giving us an unobstructed view of the white water thousands of feet below us on both sides. On the opposite valley walls we could see waterfalls hundreds of feet high suddenly emerging from the jungle only to disappear silently into the rank greenery. Despite the fact that many of the falls are hundreds of feet high, few of them are listed on maps. When the mountains are drained, most of them disappear, or are reduced to a trickle, to swell again when the next rains come.

After more than an hour of steady descent, we had dropped from 6800 feet at Pemayangtse to about 1000 feet where we crossed the green silt torrent of the Rimbihola over a recently constructed suspension bridge. Now we started right back up again, through the same botanical zones through which we had just passed. The trail was terribly steep, and the moisture, mixed with the mica, made the mud very slippery. Mercifully, we were now trekking under a cloud cover. Without it, it would have been closer to 100°F than 90°F in temperature. As it was, we were drenched in sweat. One consolation was a good view of several slow-flying racket-tailed drongos which flapped by in a way reminiscent of our own grey or Canada jay.

The next ridge was, back up at 6500 feet, a back-breaker. We quickly got into the dull-witted lead-footed plod of the trekker. Each step was heel to toe, partially because of the steepness. Every few meters there was another switch-back, so that it was not unusual to see four or five of our members with the head of one level with the feet of another, all lined up vertically facing in alternate directions.

This ridge fell away down to the next valley where another silt-laden stream frothed over the boulders. Then, incredibly, back up another 4000 foot rise before descending yet again to about 1500 feet. There we rested by a raging torrent where shelving rocks made perfect leech-free asylums where we could cool our arms and hands in the icy waters. The temptation to drink was almost irresistible, but we knew that the solids in suspension would do serious harm to our digestive systems. Our clothes were absolutely clinging to us, and we replenished lost fluids by guzzling Tang grapefruit and cold tea. The hint of the plastic from the bottle had infused the contents with a petroleum taste. We had already begun to loath our drinking containers.

Then, with mutterings of mutiny, we scaled the next valley wall until, after an alarmingly steep face, the trail intersected a paved road where we collapsed for lunch at the 14-mile post, under the watchful eye of some children, and the watchful eye of Bruce and Daku who made sure that we did not offer them any candy. Handouts seem generous, but they are very destructive to the long term well-being and pride of the mountain people. Gillian hastily put some mints back in the bag, but the bag accidentally broke. The mints on the ground no longer constituted a handout, and so they became fair game.

We left the road after passing so near to waterfalls that we benefitted from their cooling spray. The jeeps with our duffles, and carrying John who had been laid low last night, passed us. It was tempting to feel that we had been foolish not to drive from Pemayangtse to Yuksam, something, it turned out, that we could easily have done, and which we would actually do on the return trip. But at the moment we were glad to get off the pavement, as the pounding tends to heat up the inside of the climbing boots. The spongy trail was much more relaxing for the feet.

Gillian was still drained from last night's bout with the runs, and she began falling farther and farther back. I took her pack, which was substantially heavier than mine for some reason, but even my lighter pack was proving to be too much for her. Bruce was gallant enough to take the pack off her back. This helped, but the conditions were getting worse. Rain started pelting down in earnest, and our ponchos, while keeping the rain out, trapped and condensed all the ambient moisture (and our own perspiration) on the inside, and so we were drenched anyway.

Gill's water bottle was by now empty, and everyone else's was running low. We could see on the top of a hill in the distance what we thought was our destination, so no one became unduly concerned. We had consumed absolutely astonishing amounts of water, tea and juices, so Bruce's admonition to drink, drink, drink had apparently been heeded. Bruce stayed back with Gill, and I pulled ahead to try to reach Yuksam to send liquids down. Light was fading fast, and the trek had become too spread out. With no one in sight, and with no markers or directional help to guide me through the twisting jungle trail, I began to feel a sense of real panic. To make matters worse, when I reached the outskirts of the village, some children playing on a postage-stamp soccer field pointed in opposite ways at a fork in the road. Apparently, the sahibs had gone in both directions. To my dismay, what I had thought was our destination turned out to be a temple on a knoll. There was no way of telling just how much farther I still had to go. Finally, I spotted one of the drivers, squatting under an overhanging roof out of the rain. He pointed up a flooded path through some soggy fields to a cluster of yellow buildings with dull red roofs about half a mile away. Bruce's "only 20 more minutes" had turned out to be more than one and a half hours by the time I reached the Yuksam Forest Lodge. At 4:30 I sent sherpas back down to meet Gillian, Bruce, Malcolm and Dick, all of whom by this time were completely out of water. Gill drained two cups of tea in as many gulps, and promptly threw up. Nevertheless, she felt revived, and staggered into camp an hour later, well after dark. This mother hen could now relax.

The original diary entry sums it up: "This has been the

most strenuous day of my life. The backpack of 20 pounds was absurd. Tomorrow, only the rainwear stays. We've been on the trail for almost 10 hours and have only covered nine miles as the drongo flies. Not counting suspension bridges, the entire trail did not have a hundred meters of flat land. I managed not to get a single leech bite! I don't know whether to be elated or offended. It seems inconceivable that we've only gone nine miles. This has been much too difficult for the first day."

Actually, we had gone 20 miles. The vertical ascents and descents added another mile or two, and the endless switchbacks probably doubled the linear distance we had travelled. To add insult to injury, Yuksam was a full 1000 feet *lower* than Pemayangtse. We had tested our muscles to their limits, and had done absolutely nothing to acclimatize for the higher altitudes that we would now encounter.

Dinner was announced, and the 25 meter walk across the sopping grass by flashlight to the main lodge from our cabins produced three more leech victims. No meal could have been more welcome – if only our heaving stomachs could have gotten their private thoughts away from the need for more fluids. The menu included a roast of 'beef' which we all assumed to be yak, old yak at that. There were also spicy meat balls of some unidentified composition, pea soup (absolutely delicious), beans, curry, peas, carrots, cucumbers and fresh bread. Everything prepared in an adjoining smoke-filled kitchen which consisted of a working area and an open fire, an arrangement as primitive as any I had seen in Ireland.

After dinner we were introduced to our sherpas. The term refers to a specific group of hill people originally from Tibet, who live in the Khumbu Valley at the foot of Mount Everest. The first western mountaineering attacks on Everest in the 1950s passed through this valley, and the sherpas became the guides through the mountain passes they had known since time immemorial. After the exploits of Tenzing Norgay in 1953, the fame of and demand for sherpas in expeditions was great. Nor did these sturdy people disappoint. They are immensely patient, strong and friendly. They are proud of their role and are well educated in mountain skills. Above all, they are friends and guides, not beasts of burden or hirelings. The menial tasks are reserved for the porters, a ragged group of mixed ethnic backgrounds, and of totally different demeanors. We would have six sherpas assigned to the trek, and 30 porters, plus three kitchen staff.

One of the sherpas had a staphylococcus infection that had pronounced itself as a giant pustule extending from the cheek like some threatening volcano lying on its side. Further, a leech bite on his arm had become infected, so that from the elbow to the fingertips the swelling looked like an inflated rubber glove. He was found in the kitchen. Thoughts of his warming his thumb in the mashed potatoes were more than our medical team could endure. One antibiotic pill was administered along with a strict order to stay away from the food. The next morning there was hardly a trace of the infection either on the arm or on the face. No wonder that the mountain people consider most westerners to be medicine men! But the explanation for the recovery needs no supernatural intervention. We in the West take in more medicines in the course of a month than a sherpa will in a lifetime. Antibodies build up within us which reduce the effect of the medicines. No such antibodies have developed in the medicine-free systems of the sherpas, and so the impact of the "miracle drugs" is to them, indeed, miraculous. Later on in the trip, as we shall see, the shoe was on the other foot.

We retired to our rooms and rubbed down our aching limbs with DMSO, thanks to Jim Sullivan, but with suspicion from the Australian doctors who were concerned that the powerful solvent would wash any skin-borne infection or bacteria

56

deeply into the muscles. Our calves and shoulders were the sorest spots. We knew this was due in part to the loads we had been carrying. How could our porters carry their loads with such apparent ease? The answer, of course, lay in their knowledge of how to walk, and their use of a tumpline. The standard trekking load is just under 40 kilos, or about 75 pounds, plus whatever personal gear he might choose to carry. With contoured baskets and tumplines, the head and neck support about four-fifths of the weight. Any load changes your centre of gravity, and so proper walking is of fundamental importance. The smaller the gait the less the leg muscles must work, and the more natural assistance is given by the fulcrums of walking. This simple fact had become painfully obvious.

Blisters had developed before our boots "popped" to fit our feet as if custom-made. Now, moleskins were tailored into blister-sized pads to prevent further irritation and infection. Nothing is worse than feet that can't stand the punishment of the trail. That will stop you before almost anything else.

The sleeping bags had all been delivered by jeep, and tonight would be the first time we would actually sleep in them, but on a bed. To the sounds of moths bouncing off windows and walls, and the steady patter of fat rain drops, we finally fell asleep.

October 11 – As he would for the next two weeks, Sonam, our number two sherpa, brought the wake-up tea and the "washy-water" at 6:30 A.M., with breakfast of eggs and porridge at 7 A.M. From the window of the main building, we watched as our porters helped each other load up the bags and supplies that each had been assigned by Norbu, our head sherpa. Several of the porters stripped bark off a sal tree to make pliable straps which they used as the supports over their foreheads to distribute the loads in the least tiring way. With many being under five feet tall, the porters seemed

to disappear under the bags and boxes they would carry to our next camp. For the first time in its life, the longitudinal strap on my goaler's bag was useful—as a tumpline on the poor porter who was stuck with my overweight belongings. I wondered whether or not any other bag from the Port Canvas Company of Kennebunk Port, Maine, had ever or would ever see such use. How far away did Kennebunk and all it represented seem at this moment.

At 7:30 A.M. we were off, up the gently inclined trail that took us easily to the first ridge, before plunging quickly down to a log structure that crossed a lovely forest stream just below a lofty waterfall that appeared out of nowhere, its issue framed by waving ferns. Back up through tunnels cut in the vegetation, skirting rock walls that were totally clothed in luxurious moss; unseen birds sang everywhere, and our footfalls were muffled by a carpet of countless purple, yellow and mustard orchids. Their still-living mates stuck up rather than hung down from the branches against which we brushed.

Down again to the next river, across a swaying suspension bridge. Many prayer flags fluttered from its cables. A water ouzel guarded a magic pool which was fed by yet another waterfall springing from a jungle source. In addition to the orchids, there were wild exotic fruits and nuts that littered the path, and unseen overhead in the canopy of the forest, troops of monkeys monitored our progress with great commotion. The vegetation was wondrously lush, for we were now climbing through our first cloud forest.

The mid-elevation forest literally combs the moisture out of the air. Droplets that form clouds or fog are too light to fall to the ground. Instead, the droplets are blown against the foliage where they coalesce along the sharp edges of the leaves, running together until they drip to the ground below. The 'rain' therefore is not rain at all. The plants that are typical of this forest zone have adapted to an ecological niche in which so much moisture is suspended in the air that the need has disappeared for a ground-level or underground moisture-gathering root system. Instead, this is replaced by mechanisms designed to draw water straight from the clouds. The epiphytes, mosses, ferns, orchids and other highly specialized plants sprout from the elbows of branches, or drape the trunks and limbs in a hairy garb. These arboreal plants are not, as a rule, parasites. Rather than deriving sustenance from their hosts, or at the expense of their hosts, they merely use the larger trees as platforms from which to drink from the clouds that swirl around them even in the dry season.

This same moisture also makes for a perfect leech habitat. Leeches are heat-seeking machines. Suspended by their sucker-like foot from the underside of a leaf, they seem to "sniff" the air for a passing body. When walking in a line, the first trekker catches the leech's attention, the second walker brings the leech to the "ready" state, and, like the third-man-on-the-match of trench warfare infamy, the third trekker finds a leech dropping onto him. At least, so it seemed. The third man received more than his share of leech bites. It may also have been a case of body chemistry. Just as two people can walk through the same cloud of black flies or mosquitos and receive totally different bites, so too can individuals walk the same path and receive different leech attacks. I received none; Malcolm received 17 in one day.

We had covered a lot of ground before our first rest stop one hour and forty-five minutes after leaving Yuksam. The trail had begun to degenerate, and we were by now picking our steps more carefully than before. Frequently, the path of least resistance took us right along the retaining wall of stones that had been placed along the very edge of the path. It was something of a jolt to realise that we were walking on slippery rocks within a shoe's width of a several hundred foot plunge into the jungle below.

Jungle leech walking prior to being stepped on.

We stopped for lunch at 11 A.M., and had the opportunity of watching the cooks prepare a feast for 50 people on two open fires. Tea, curried chicken, chapatis, apples, bananas, jam and delicious goat cheese brought back some of the strength that we had lost. Without being too conscious of it, we had been climbing steadily and were now at about 7500 feet, the highest point so far on the trip. Several members of the group were beginning to puff a little. The view from our

lunch spot was of the cloud forest and a stream far below. The sounds of birds and of waterfalls were all around us. Unfortunately, the spot was also "very leechy" according to Daku, and indeed we saw several that were easily three inches long. Admittedly, they only have to eat once every two or three weeks, but what did they do before tasty trekkers came along?

The afternoon trek was as bad or worse than what we had experienced yesterday, but it was at least mercifully short.

At 2:45 P.M. we reached Bahkim Forest Rest House at 9000 feet exactly. We had spent the last two hours climbing straight up and had covered perhaps a mile. The Rest House was a square two-storeyed yellow building. The flat front looked out over a small patio, and offered a breathtaking view of dozens of ridges interlocking in shades of deep blues and purples with the cloud blanketing the depths. It was with a sense of accomplishment that we realised that we had actually climbed up and down these same ridges during the last two days.

The vegetation had begun to change as we gained altitude. There were more pines and firs, and several plants had long waxy holly-like leaves. There was still the occasional bamboo thicket of riotous green, but the species was much smaller than the giant members we had seen below Pemayangtse. The most interesting flora, to my mind, were various species of nuts of the acorn type which, not surprisingly, abounded in the oak forests. Some were covered in a layered dull green pulp in which the pattern looked like roof shingles. From the inch and a half cover there emerged a three-quarter inch nut. Another species, with smaller acorns, grew like a cluster of fungus with the tips of the nut barely visible at the openings.

The most astonishing of all was a large pale yellow nut (perhaps still unripe) in which the dirty green folded and flattened cover, by an incredible example of concealing mimicry, looked exactly like fresh yak droppings! They also smelled most foul when they began rotting. How wondrous are the ways of nature....

Late in the afternoon we finally reached the jungle lodge of Bahkim, perched on a small clearing on the steep slope of the hill. In front lay the precipitous valley with side spurs meshing like teeth in verdant gears. Behind was a mammoth boulder with ferns cascading over the top. The forest had

60

been so thick that we had no visual clue that we had been approaching our destination. As we rounded what turned out to be the last spur, we had been greeted by a horse. This meant man, and it was a welcome omen. Everyone was exhausted. "Why are we abusing our bodies this way?" I asked in my diary. The legs just seized up when you sat. Contemplating our aches and spasms, we thought back on this day during which we had learned to hate those sections of the path which led down, wrenching your knees, but more importantly which reclaim all the altitude you had so laboriously gained. On the return trip, the up-paths were to become equally detestable. And we learned to hate the scree that gave as much footing as would ball bearings. Considerable sections of the 'path' were stream beds, and that at least helped keep the feet cool. Now that we were at 9000 feet, emotions began to heighten, and words like "hate" crept into our vocabulary.

Even at this altitude we were dripping with perspiration. Watching a large dark Himalayan squirrel rummaging around under our window made us feel tired. And then the temperatures began to drop alarmingly. Within minutes we could see our breath, and we were now not only wet but also cold. The porters had not yet arrived with the rest of the duffle bags, but Mickey's was there. Throwing fashion to the winds, we shared whatever dry and warm clothes we could. Lethargy was setting in, and the same forests that earlier in the day had been filled with birds of erudite Latin names were now filled with nothing but members of the "who-gives-a-shit" species. Even their calls were annoying. The discovery of a leech bite would have made things even worse, but we were now above the leech line, and I had come through unscathed. I do not like the sight of my own blood.

Everyone rubbed down with DMSO and our limbs were on fire. The aches and pains, however, were relatively few.

It was pitch black by 6 P.M., and our candles did little except to add atmosphere. Dinner around the huge (How did they ever get it up here!) polished wooden table was by kerosene lamp. The light cast sharply contrasting shadows on all our faces, and we all looked like shipwrecked detritus. The craggy, whiskered faces of Peter, Dick and Kendall, three-fifths of our medical team, were all the more ominous as they forcefully argued against trying to reach Dzongri, as per

Eurasian Goldfinch
Carduelis carduelis

our schedule, the next day. At 13,000 feet, a 5000 foot gain in one day, we would be courting disaster. Mountain sickness, Peter intoned, was insidious. It manifested itself 36 to 48 hours after the altitude has already unbalanced your blood system. The only cure is rapid descent, but the terrain mitigated against such an evacuation.

According to the sherpas and Daku, there was one other unnamed camp site we could reach at about 12,000 feet, but there was no water there. This meant that our supply would have to be shouldered up by some porters who were at this stage showing increasing signs of edginess. They knew that we were heading into late snow, and many of them were barefoot. The soles of their feet had long since been insulated with thick callouses, but nevertheless, plodding at altitude through the snow with tanks of water on your back could hardly be considered ideal working conditions, even for the handsome pay (about a dollar fifty a day) they would receive. It was decided that we would strike out for "Lower" Dzongri at the crack of dawn. This way we could acclimatize more slowly. Under optimum conditions it is preferable to climb a thousand feet per day above 10,000 feet. From sea level to 10,000 feet causes no problems, but above that limit changes can be severe.

On the table were lumps of yogurt, tomato soup, rice with coriander, nuts and raisins, dahl, cubes of meat, curried potatoes, and tinned peaches. The tea and hot chocolate, however, were both undrinkable. Brushing your teeth was out, and there was no water in the toilets. We stumbled into our sleeping bags like hamburgers, all dressed. John broke the Guinness Book of Records for snore decibels. Absolutely incredible.

October 12 – Day three of the trek: Washy-water and wake-up tea arrived on schedule at 5:30, breakfast at 6:15, and on the trail an hour later. The path cut up behind the lodge, with a series of switch-backs which diminished the grade but added distance. For the first time, we were made aware of what came to be called "Sherpa Shortcuts" – straight up the line of direct ascent. Using an easy trail must be below their dignity. The day was warm and sunny. We had left the clouds in the valleys, and the opposite hills shimmered in the brilliant clear light. The forest changed every few hundred feet, and as the trees thinned, we were face to face with the peaks we had come to see. Blindingly white against the blue sky, they surpassed anything I had ever dreamed of. Kipling, in *Kim*, described it: "Above them, still enormously above them, earth towered away to the snow line…Above these again, changeless since the world's beginning, but changing to every mood of sun and cloud, lay out the eternal snow."

Our views were framed by moss-draped trees, and our horizon precluded a full sweep. Nevertheless, in all their majesty, here was *alaya* (the abode or home) of *hima* (the snow). The greatest mountain range in the world, 1700 miles long, from 100 to 150 miles wide, straddling eight countries on the modern map, and a hundred kingdoms from the pages of history – here indeed was the home of the snows. Everest, K2 and Kangchenjunga are all over 28,000 feet; 13 other peaks top 26,000 feet; there are scores over 20,000 feet, and hundreds, perhaps thousands higher than Mont Blanc. The 'hills' from 6000 to 8000 feet are so numerous they have never been counted or even named.

An hour out of Bahkim we came upon the Tibetan refugee village of Tzokha, a scattering of a dozen wooden huts, unkempt fields, a maze of paths, chortons and fluttering flags. A moss-rimmed depression served as a catchment for water. The degree of purity was questioned in direct ratio to the amount of suspicious red and gree algae which encroached on the reflections on the surface. This was, to say the very least, an isolated outpost of civilization. Apart from two seasonally inhabited thatched bamboo jungle huts and the refuges of stone where we would stop at Dzongri and Thangshing, this was the last sign of human habitation. From here on in we were walking back through the geologic millennia. But even in its isolation, Tzokha had its compensations. The view down the valley was beautiful, the air was crisp, the stark pines whispered against a spectacular backdrop, and there were jungle crows and ravens to stand sentinel. Above all, the Tzokhanese were free from persecution. Sonam's mother and siblings live here, and we would visit with them on our descent.

We were now well into the rhododendron forests, through which a corduroy road had been laid intermittently for about half a mile. It made the walking much easier, as the ground was very muddy. The air was cool, and yet even now at 11,000 feet we were moist with perspiration.

With our shortened itinerary, we stopped for an early lunch around 9:45 in a forest clearing where the mosses and stumps and fallen logs combined to make wonderful contoured couches and armchairs. The smoke of our fire billowed serenely blue-grey to seep out through the trees for a momentary flash of brilliance before dissipating into the realms of memories. Pea-filled chapatis, beans, goat cheese, hard-boiled eggs – our lunch was interrupted by a family with their *zums* and *zohs,* crosses between yaks and cattle, whose tinkling bells seemed much more appropriate than the infernal throbbing of an Indian army helicopter that had followed us, or at least followed our trail for over an hour. The thought had crossed our minds that the authorities had been trying to find us to deliver some unwanted message.

The porters sat watching on logs and perched on stumps, and smoked a suspicious-smelling wild tobacco which we assumed was not addictive if we stood downwind. They could easily have been a convocation of forest elves.

After lunch the trail climbed very precipitously, and there began to be patches of corn snow among the rhododendrons. "Thank God this isn't spring," quipped Kendall, "or else Dave would stop to take pictures of the flowers..." The wry comment was a good-natured dig. I was snapping dozens of close-ups of ferns, leaf patterns, bark, berries, mosses,

A tired rhododendron with hinged leaves so they can shed the snow.

mushrooms and other minutiae. Had the rhododendrons been in bloom, I would have been there still! There are an estimated 155,000 species of flowering tropical plants in the world, of which 35,000 are found in Asia. There are also 20,000 of the world's 90,000 species of fungus in Asia. I decided the challenge for the potential botanist was too exhausting.

Nevertheless, rhododendrons could become a passion, as they had been for Sir Joseph Dalton Hooker, one of the most eminent nineteenth century naturalists, who had travelled through the Himalayas studying plant distribution and evolution. From 1848 to 1850 he spent more time in Sikkim than he had bargained for because he refused to leave his close friend, Mr. Campbell, who was being held a political prisoner by the Sikkimese. (As a result, the British felt the need to punish the local ruler, and as Britannia ruled the waves, she could waive the rules. London snatched away that portion of the land which became the Darjeeling area to be annexed to India proper. That'll teach 'em!)

Dalton was overwhelmed by the diversity of the rhododendrons. Their convoluted branches wove a matrix over the hills like so many vegetable Laocöons. What he found was quite unexpected: no fewer than 22 new species, all of which he drew for his hand-coloured lithographs to illustrate his lavish folio *The Rhododendrons of Sikkim-Himalaya*. While still in exile in 1849 the first parts of the book were published under the watchful eye of his father, Sir William, who was the director of Kew Gardens. In that year, Sir Joseph could write with exuberance: "All the Indian world is in love with my Rhododendron book!" Little wonder. The definitive *Pantologia or New Cyclopedia*, as late as 1813, had listed a grand total of 10 species, "chiefly native to the Alps and of Siberia; one or two indigenous to America," and gave a description of six species.

By now, my head had begun pounding with such force that I actually stopped to see if there was a woodpecker nearby. It was frightening to realize that the throbbing was actually coming from my own body. It probably would have been a good idea to rest, but the weather was turning nasty and there was a need to press on. It was easier to pretend that I had a woodpecker as a companion for the rest of the way.

At 12:50 we reached the clearing of Lower Dzongri, a knoll at about 12,000 feet. The ground was already a quagmire, and getting worse by the minute in the downpour of snow and slush. Mickey, in her hiking shorts, was almost as underdressed as many of the porters. The sherpas put up our sky blue tents in incredibly short time, and we all claimed our own to try to warm up, but without luck. We finally bundled four to a tent to keep out the cold, and slept fitfully until 6 P.M. In the pitch blackness, we slogged by flashlight through the swamp, every step crashing through the thin ice into ankle-deep water and ooze, to the large mess tent. It was still snowing, and it was bitterly cold. So this is how Oates felt.

We sat on canvas three-legged camp stools, strategically placed out of the way of the running leaks in the tent roof, huddled around the fire, drank soup, ate rice and curry with chopsticks (quite a feat with numb fingers) and rejected the water which was the colour of weak tea.

Shooting cholic pains prompted me to take two Lomotil tablets, which, as they proved very effective, turned out to be a mistake. Voiding bodily wastes at altitude is essential if mountain sickness is to be avoided.

The day that had started off so well had become physically and mentally exhausting. Even writing was difficult. Looking back on the diary, spelling had become atrocious, and good grammar "had went." We had gone from 95°F to 25°F, and from 800 feet to over 12,000 feet in just under two days. We were cold, wet and miserable. The tent floor felt like a water bed, and actually gurgled when you put pressure on any given spot. If tomorrow's weather is awful, the barefoot porters will revolt. They won't carry on to Dzongri in the snow. If this is "moderate trekking," what in the world is "difficult"?

At 7:45 P.M. I climbed into my sleeping bag for the first time not on a bed, and reflected that half a world away it was Canadian Thanksgiving. We have much to be thankful for.

October 13 – Day four of the trek – And I quote: "We slept fully clothed plus balaclava and gloves. The snow kept coming down. This is really stupid. We are simply not equipped for this kind of thing. My sinuses hurt more than I have ever experienced; it's awful just to move my eyes. The alarm clock was the terrible Himalayan hack of the sherpas and porters, many of whom are barefoot and without ground sheets. I started the morning with a Lomotil and two 222s. This is the first time this trek has been done by Mountain Travel, and the length and difficulty of the stages are too much, and the weather has caught them by surprise. This is really dumb. This is being written at 5:30 A.M., so perhaps my mood colours what I'm recording, but at this moment I find it hard to believe that someday I'll look back on this part of the trip as a fun or positive experience. This verges on masochism. It is really stupid."

The sun, however, was shining, and soon warmed the tents sufficiently to thaw the flap zippers, and to allow sheets of snow to slide off the roof just as I emerged. The sherpas had chopped holes in the ice to get ground water which they were boiling over a leaping fire. Boiling might kill bacteria, but the thought crossed our minds that at this altitude, the boiling water might well be below the boiling point of bugs. Germ-free or not, only a strainer, or better yet a filter, could remove the lumps and clear up the peat-brown colour.

Breakfast at 7 A.M., and on the trail by 7:25. We were climbing a ridge paralleling a vast barrier of mountains across the valley on our right hand side. We could see on their flanks a dusting of last night's snow well below the tree line, up through rhododendrons for another mile or so, crossing and recrossing the tree line, marching over snow fields with grey soggy patches of slush always, it seemed, right in our path.

The tree line itself is influenced by exposure, by rain and above all by temperature, specifically summer, not winter temperature. The line corresponds with the 50°F isotherm for July, the warmest month. The highest trees are the fir (*Abies spectabilis*), the birch (*Betula utilis*), and the large rhododendrons (*Rhododendron campanulatum, R. hodgsonii, R. grande,* and *R. barbatum*). Above that, there is a zone of Alpine scrub – the dwarf rhododendrons (*R. setosum, R. anthopogon* and *R. nivale*) and several low junipers. Increased exposure to wind and rain lowers the tree line to about 11,000 feet, but elsewhere in this area it is clearly defined at approximately 12,000 feet.

The hinged leaves of the rhododendrons buckled under the weight of the six inches of snow, allowing the load to slip harmlessly off the plant which otherwise would have been in danger of losing its leaves. The snowy branches and the dark waxy foliage were exquisite against the looming peaks.

The blue sky, however, was soon overwhelmed by masses of thick cloud that welled up from far below. By 10 A.M. we were in a blizzard. The visibility was reduced to a few meters, and we groped up steep hills over a pass of 15,300 feet before picking our way down to a small, quasi-protected hollow, surrounded by a split-rail fence and containing a low stone hut, mostly buried in the snows that had already caved in one of the walls and collapsed part of the roof. This was Dzongri, a place that makes me feel sick every time I hear its name.

Gillian was moving very slowly, so she, Kendall and I arrived almost 45 minutes after the leaders. Mickey was already in her tent, but not doing very well. The rest of us sat around cooking our boots over the fire. We had been using them as skis during the descent, and the water was not steaming out of their outer surfaces. The insides were, happily, bone dry. We had lunch of poori and sardines. This, plus the acrid smoke from the resinous wood fire that filled the room before seeping out through the dry walls and the shakes in the roof, was too much for Gillian. She began serious vomiting and diarrhoea. Kendall looked after his first case this trip of mountain sickness.

I thought she would be very foolish to carry on tomorrow for even though we would drop 1000 feet, we would have to climb over a 15,600 foot pass to get to Thangshing, and more importantly, we would be another full day into the mountains, a full day further away from help. If necessary, she could stay at Dzongri to acclimatize for another day or two, or until she was strong enough to walk, and could then catch up with us. As it turned out, it was Mickey about whom we should have been worried.

The camp consisted of two huts placed on a built-up area, all arranged along the same axis. The kitchen was located in the space between the two buildings which had been covered over. The walls were of well-dressed blocks of local stone, perhaps eight inches by ten inches, piled on top of each other in parallel rows without any mortar. The Incas would have snorted. The pitch of the roof was very slight, the whole being supported by massive timbers, and covered with shakes of pine or fir, many at least three and four feet long. At the apex of the roof, the room was not more than six and a half feet, and where the roof met the walls, not five feet. The interior was divided by a dry wall which did not attempt to follow the peak of the roof line. Each chamber was twenty-five by fifteen feet, with a low door, a small window and a floor of large planks. In the centre, a pit had been left in which the fire was laid. After a thousand years of use, it would seem reasonable that an indigenous design appropriate for the hostile environment would have evolved. The dry walls and the shakes might let the smoke out, but they also let the cold in. And the slight slope of the roof did not shed snow properly, nor was there any inside buttressing at ground level. Not surprisingly, this shed, not yet two years old, was already well on its way to being a ruin. The roof had collapsed, the timbers had been rearranged and the exterior wall had buckled. Even the interior dividing wall had fallen, lying about like a terminal moraine of some retreated glacier. As Hamish Macaulay, my partner in Montreal, and an experienced mountaineer in his own right, had said, "You'll be seeing what the Swiss were like a thousand years ago."

The overpowering memory of such huts was, simply, smoke, thick acrid choking smoke that permeated your clothes and saturated your skin and hair. In his wonderful book, *Arun*, Edward W. Cronin, Jr., described having asked a sherpa why they endured the smoke. "It feels good," came the answer. From our urban, polluted vantage point, it is difficult to understand that smoke "feels good" to those people by whom the clean, endless air of the Himalayas is taken for granted. Fire, above everything else, represents a man-made environment, something on a human rather than a divine scale. It, by extension, can mean society, friendship, food, security, even life or death. These overtones are more important perhaps than mere warmth. The smoky interiors which to us are choking are sought out by these mountain people for all these reasons. The psychological explanation is certainly more valid than the unacceptable answer that the mountain tribes never invented or borrowed something as simple as a chimney, or its lack – a hole in the roof. Even in the lowlands, where corrugated tin has replaced thatch, the smoke is still allowed to seep out of the dented ends of the houses because the inhabitants have borrowed only selectively from the twentieth century.

And the effects of smoky interiors on the health standards have been grave. Conjunctivitis is endemic, and, as Kipling wrote: "The women of the smoky huts ... were unlovely and unclean, wives of many husbands, and afflicted with goitre."

To escape the smoke I crouched through the low door out into the snow. A small mountain stream gurgled down towards and under a plank-walled outhouse. Two ravens coughed as they stood guard, a wren flitted around the stacked fire wood, and a large black dog investigated. Obviously it had been he who was responsible for the "snow leopard" tracks we had seen in the snow. Just then a yak train passed through down from higher levels where the conditions were even worse. Despite their bulk the animals are very agile, leaping over turnstiles and off four-foot ledges with abandon.

As the altitude increases, tempers shorten. Eric Shipton and Sir Edmund Hillary both had told us of this. Petty annoyances at sea level become causes for justifiable homicide at altitude. Just such a case now took place.

By common consent, John was a crashing bore who monopolized every conversation with endless non-related anecdotes, poorly told, in an unfortunately unpleasing voice and with a mannerism of interspersing an affected little cough every few words. He also breathed in the middle, never the end of a sentence, so that no one could cut in. A plethora of minute detail afflicted even the simplest tale and rendered it tedious. He was well launched into another voyage of self-praise about his trip to England to join some regiment (about which he gave the names of officers and the battles in which they had fought) to oversee some highly detailed project (which he detailed highly), travelling on the *Scythia,* which he added, parenthetically, "was a converted P. & O. liner."

That did it. Something snapped, and I could hold back no longer. "Goddammit," I fairly screamed, "she was a Cunarder. She was not a P. & O. She ended in "ia," a province of ancient Rome. *Carpathia, Saxonia, Carmenia, Ivernia, Franconia,* – they were all "ia" and they were all Cunarders!" Spontaneously, the rest of his captive audience broke into cheers. Unfazed, John blinked: "I stand corrected," and launched forth again, undaunted, but this time to a rapidly shrinking group. As in animal art, if obsessive detail is part of your affliction, then make sure that the detail is either accurate or that your audience is uneducated. Especially at altitude.

My diary continues: "It's now 3:15 P.M., and it has begun pouring with rain. I would be delighted to call the whole trek off. We're just too close to the limits of our endurance, especially with most of us suffering in varying degrees with mountain sickness. At supper I got up too quickly from my sleeping bag and came down with an amazing case of the shakes. I thought my teeth would fall out. Up to the dinner lodge – the low, heavy smoky atmosphere almost did me in. I managed to down soup and a cup of Ovaltine. Then back to my tent under escort by Kendall. A hot water bottle helped."

Kipling: "'But the food is very bad,' Kim growled, 'and we walk as though we were mad – or English. It freezes at night, too!'

'A little, maybe, but only enough to make old bones rejoice in the sun. We must not always delight in the soft beds and rich food.'"

Even the stoicism of Kipling's lama was scant consolation. Dzongri had already become a four letter word.

October 14 – Day five of the trek – My sinuses and headache woke me every half hour on the half hour. With each bout of consciousness I moved from my side to my back to my other side and back again trying to find some relief from the pounding. I wanted to gouge my eyes out, to squeeze them and tell them to stop hurting me. Before going to sleep I had carefully arranged everything – tissues, pills, Tang-flavoured water and the flashlight – where I could reach them without having to get out of the sleeping bag. Unfortunately, the scheme was predicated on my being able to find the flashlight, which in turn required far more concentration than I could possibly muster under the circumstances. At 4:30 I finally found the light and with it the 222s. With codeine I was able to sleep until 6 A.M. when tea came around. I passed on the washy-water which was stone-cold by the time I struggled to the plastic bucket. Instead, I welcomed a second cup of tea when Sonam's welcomed shadow darkened my tent roof again.

I could hear Gillian and Mickey a couple of tents away, so I assumed they were both feeling better. The Australian doctors were very surprised that the girls had been prescribed "the Pill" as both the pill and the altitude tend to reinforce the tendency for thrombosis. Gillian felt that her trouble was largely a reaction against the drugs. In any event, Kendall and Dick were quite insistent that they dispose of the remaining pills immediately.

We forced ourselves to eat breakfast in that infernal smoke-filled hut, and by now realized just how much we detested the tin plates which invariably remained frozen, quickly congealing every warm thing that was placed on them. Fried eggs turned to India rubber. And the scraping of the knives across their scotched surface was like nails being dragged down the blackboard. The altitude seemed to heighten our senses.

We had hoped to see the legendary view from Dzongri. The direct quote from the official tourist brochure whets the appetite: "Dzongri offers you the most fascinating close-up view of the Khangchendzonga massif. Immediately opposite rises Pandim, 21,958 feet, cloaked in thick ice-hood. To the left appears the deep gap of Goecha La. To the west over the gentle slopes of Dzongri rises the long outline of the Khungla ridge. The sunset from Dzongri is flamboyant and breathtaking. You spend the day exploring the splendours of the Himalayas and perhaps ride on a yak."

We did not see a single thing. Rather than a morning of "flamboyant and breathtaking" views, we were in for a morning of unrelenting self-abuse. We took off at 7:30 directly up a 45 degree slope to a ridge at over 14,500 feet. We were totally enveloped by clouds, and snow squalls plagued our every step as we headed across acres of boulders, sticking up like slippery islands in an endless swamp of ice and snow and slush. As the temperatures rose, the snows melted and the whole mountainside was in flood. "You will pass by gorgeous valleys of flowers, cool mountain rivulets, forests with chirping birds..." continues the tourist brochure.

We bounded from stone to stone for over an hour at altitudes ranging from over 15,000 feet down to just under 14,000 feet. The trail then suddenly plunged over the end of a mountain spur, down through snow-covered rhododendrons. The path was a shoot of sliding mud and water. This cruel joke of a path combined the least desirable features of Verdun trench warfare and a Jurassian farmyard in which the ooze never dries or quite deodorizes.

But then, suddenly, the clouds dispersed, and directly across from us were the mountains, blindingly white against the blue sky, magnificently framed by the twisted branches of the rhododendrons, the beards of moss that draped their branches, and the tall pines on hillsides so steep that the lofty crown of one tree reached the roots of its neighbour above. The overpowering force of the scene made the trekking seem easier.

The porters, who had long since passed us, already had the

69

fires burning and the water for our tea boiling along the trail at perhaps the most enchanting spot on the entire trip. We picked our way down through a dense festooned forest, absolutely filled "with chirping birds" that refused to show themselves, and came out onto a clearing strewn with large boulders completely enveloped in beautiful moss and lichen. Through this paradise a glacial stream slid in satin sheets over rocks to pools where the waters caught their breath before racing on in foam and froth over rapids and falls around the bend and out of sight. The therapeutic value of rushing rivers cannot be overstated.

Norbu gathered handfuls of what he called "blue raspberries," which they obviously were not. About the size of monster blueberries, they were the colour of a bluebird's back, fading to blue-white at the bottom. They were icy cold and tasted delicately of wintergreen. Nothing could have been more delicious at 11,500 feet in the cool, clean air, and with the blessed warmth of the sun soaking into every pore.

While we all sprawled out on the moss, catching up on our diaries, massaging sore feet, and drying socks on the warm stones, the porters lounged around, smoking and chatting, or bending to collect little leaves of alpine plants that Daku said might well come in handy "if we need some mountain medicines."

Gillian and I felt rejuvenated, but Mickey was really under the weather. She slept too heavily, and we had trouble getting her started again. Under the prodding of the doctors and of Bruce, we all forced ourselves to drink vast quantities of tea and fruit juices. We thought we would vomit. We all agreed that we would never knowingly have brought any of the children on this trek. For Peter and his heart, it would have been foolhardy. If anything had gone wrong, the responsibility would have been horrific.

After lunch we crossed the stream, and climbed up along the opposite bank through moss-dripping rhododendrons, up through bogs and hummocks and giant boulders. Mickey was moving very slowly, and the concern for her well-being was beginning to show on everyone's face. She was stopping frequently, and, almost as if pleading for mercy, categorically refused to take any more fluids.

By the time we broke over a ridge into a vast U-shaped valley, high clouds had already blotted out the sun. Incongruously, there was a short winding path of white stones not 25 yards long that led unexpectedly to another low slung, dry wall hut with an undulating roof line of shakes. A tall Tibetan prayer flag broadcast its endless OM MANI PADME HUMS on the winds which were now to our backs. Masses of clouds were boiling just below the ridge as if some malevolent army was waiting to charge into our sanctuary. The sherpas had already set up our tents on flat dry land, and the bluish smoke seeping out through the roof of the hut told of warmth and probably of tea. A small canal had been dug to intercept any water that might have percolated down onto our campsite, carrying the run-off in defiance of the laws of gravity at right angles to the lie of the land, and under the outhouse perched stategically at the point where our private waterway emptied – no longer unsullied – into the torrent where we had shared the valley since lunch. Rising above the stream were jagged cliffs. Their aprons were slopes of house-sized blocks, several of which, lacking moss, were obviously of recent arrival. It was comforting that all of them were on the side of the stream opposite the camp. Looking up the valley, to the right side were tongues of rododendron forests that linked the valley floor with the snow line. And arched above from the cliffs on the one hand to the snow on the other was an opaque ceiling of cloud, depressing us, oppressing us, and blotting out any view or even hint of the mountains that we knew must be there.

Towards the pass above Dzongri
15,300 feet in the snow

71

Mickey was doing very poorly, and was sent to her tent. The thought of the low, dark, smoke-filled hut made us all nauseous, and the thought of supper was almost more than we could bear. We promised ourselves that, if we were to escape from this worthwhile experience alive, we would treat ourselves to a meal at the three-star restaurant of René Varaud. If only the sun would shine, everything would feel so much better.

Within minutes of our arrival, it began snowing with a vengeance. We're having rotten luck; Daku said that she had never seen weather like this so late in the year. All the porters and sherpas gleefully agreed that this was indeed a disaster.

The doctors worked on Mickey all afternoon, but she was not well enough to attempt to get up for a meal, no matter how needed the food might be. Basically, she was now immobile, in excruciating pain, and on the verge of being delirious. She confided to Gillian about what she wanted done if she were to die, and generally was beyond caring. The rest of us spent another smoke-filled dinner keeping our thoughts quite to ourselves. The camp was not as active as it had been earlier because with our reduced amount of food – several days' worth having already been eaten – several of the porters had been released and they had headed back to lower climes, back to their smoke-filled huts and to their way of life little influenced by the twentieth century.

Of great interest was the record book that had to be filled in by each expedition, signifying that the porters had received full compensation for their work. Their names were written out in full, almost all by the sirdar, for the overwhelming majority of the porters, unlike the sherpas, were illiterate. A revenue stamp was placed after their name, and the individual would confirm receipt by making a thumb print over the stamp. Thomas Bewick would have been pleased...

We also noted that the government department of forests employs a collector of firewood, and that we were being charged for the amount that we had been burning. Apparently every government hut is restocked after a trek moves through so that no one comes to a camp without the insurance policy of dry fuel.

Dick was sitting on his canvas stool in the corner, listening to a cassette of a hauntingly lovely Mozart flute concerto. The melody seeped with the smoke over the interior dividing wall into the section where the support staff was relaxing after their evening meal. Mozart had a profound and immediate affect on the mountaineers whose lighthearted chatter abruptly stopped. Up until that time, this had been a relatively normal end to an exhausting day. I'll never forget what happened.

That night held one of the most profound experiences of my life. We had gone to supper in the dark, the fog and the snow. The welcome fire almost chapped our faces and hands, and made the clothes and boots exposed to the flame extremely hot to the touch. Our backs were nevertheless frozen. Rice, curry, tea, vegetables, meat – the kitchen had again done wonders, but we were not in a condition to appreciate it. We coaxed the fire into new life and sat around talking quietly or listening rather than having to face the snowy walk back to our freezing tents.

About 9:30 the door opened, and in filed sherpas and remaining porters – about 30 in all. Squatting around the campfire's embers, they sang and some danced the songs of the Himalayas, music a thousand years old. The flames cast flickering shadows across their brown faces, highlighting cheeks and liquid eyes. The muscles in their feet and toes, barefoot in this untravelled world, were etched by the fire light, the resinous smoke, the glowing coals, the hand-clapped rhythms, the faces – it was overpowering. We were transported back a millennium.

And then the music stopped. We were absolutely drained emotionally. We finally bade our porters goodnight and stepped out into a hard freeze. The clouds had given way to unfamiliar constellations, and looming, towering, floating ethereally overhead was Pandim. We put our arms around each other and wept.

Said Kim, "Surely the Gods live here."

October 15 – Day six of the trek – To my disappointment I awoke at 2:30 A.M. with a 222 headache and a monumental sinus attack. I had hoped against hope that I would by now have become acclimatized. After the 222s I slept until 6 A.M. and sweated through very vivid dreams. There was an instant replay of my son Gordon's two goals against Selwyn House and his four against Collège des Etudistes. Perhaps the outside temperature reminded me of the deep-freeze that is the ice rink at Lower Canada College. Then came the frustration and final triumph, after a long afternoon together, of little David learning to catch a ball properly. I shared Cynthia's agony of waiting to hear back from Princeton as to whether or not she had been accepted. The dream about universities may have been caused by Daku's having asked about student loans at Dartmouth to which her son had applied for fall '81. Then there was Sarah, laughing in her too-big glasses, unruly hair and her Study School uniform.

The dream and the lie of the tent did not make for a sound sleep. Not being on level ground, my sleeping bag kept answering the call of gravity, slipping off the under sheet, and depositing me in the corner among my shambled belongings. Caterpillar-like I would hump back to temporary equilibrium.

The promise of last night failed to deliver at dawn. The high clouds obscured the peaks, so all we could see were the lower portions of our valley's walls. At least the birds were

THANGSHING
CAMP 12,300'

singing, especially the pipits. The fact that everything was frozen hard did not seem to dampen their exuberance.

Breakfast conversation resolved around subjects that at sea level would have been considered too personal. At altitude, however, and in the constant presence of danger, the members of a group such as ours lose all their inhibitions. The health of one person affects the progress – and even the safety – of the whole trek, and so Mickey's vital signs were cause for common concern. Our health was even more important in view of the fact that we were not sure exactly where or how high the next camp was. Some thought that it was two hours away, others thought four hours; some claimed that it was at 14,000 feet, others at 16,000 feet. Originally, the itinerary called for the classic "climb high – sleep low" approach. We would make a dash for the Goecha La at 16,800 feet, and descend to 14,000 feet to spend the night. If, as it appeared, the maps had reversed the last two camps, we would be sleeping at over 15,000 feet, something that might cause real problems for anyone on the verge of acute mountain sickness. The government maps were of little use. Reliability of the information was highly questionable, for the detailed surveys simply had never been done.

In all events, Mickey would not be able to carry on. The night before, she had pleaded to be left behind, and this morning Bruce and the doctors conferred, did an examination and unanimously agreed that, in light of her not being in critical danger, it would be best for her to stay at Thangshing with Norbu and a porter. She would be at a relatively low altitude, sure of fire and warmth, in good hands, and able to let nature take its course for acclimatization. The rest of us would proceed, and return to fetch her in two days. As for Mickey herself, she was beyond caring.

After breakfast, the ground fog began to lift. As I was walking back to my tent I was stopped in my tracks by a reflection in a puddle. There was the summit of Pandim. I looked up, and towering two miles above was the tip of the sacred mountain floating, unanchored to earth or reality, above the broad band of mist that completely blotted out any view of the lower portions of the massive bulk. In its own way, the impact matched our starlit view of last night.

Then, the promise of last night *was* delivered. The sun burned off the clouds, and a glorious sunrise overwhelmed us. Pandim was our first giant peak. The soft, almost voluptuous contours of the eternal snows contrast vividly with the stark geometrics of the black cliffs and fractured rock faces. From our valley vantage point, it was easy to fantasize about routes to the top. Your eye would start to trace a line of attack up the ridges, slanting across snow fields, easily picking your way between the crevasses as glaciers spilled over a hidden rock barrier. But invariably, even your fantasies had to admit that your path had run into a treacherous cul-de-sac, and you would have to start over. To a competent climber, the ascent probably would not prove unduly difficult, but Pandim remains unclimbed. As the Sacred Mountain of the Sikkimese, the ex-king felt that he should be the first to conquer it, one of the many plans thwarted by the loss of his crown to Indian democracy. Pandim is too wonderful to fall to a man's (even a king's) ambition. Out of respect, I hope that any future attempt will stop 50 feet below the summit. Pandim should be left "in mysterium tremendum."

As the sun rose, the head of the valley was completely damned by a shimmering, brilliant wall of snow. Stretching our view, and trending up to the left behind the near still black cliffs was the titanic massif of Kangchenjunga. It was incredible. Then the sun rose at our backs over some critical ridge or peak, and the valley was flooded in light. It was as if the dam of Kangchenjunga had burst. The brooding cliffs were now bathed in golden light, and the frost crystal that had embraced the lichen and leaves of the dwarf junipers began a retreat. The line coincided exactly with the advancing rays of the new day. The snowy rhododendrons began shedding their unseasonal burden, and the hinged leaves flexed upwards. Small birds were singing everywhere. The only unhappy note was Mickey.

The sherpas struck camp with their usual dispatch, and, after an emotional farewell at Mickey's lonely tent, we started up the valley at 8:20. The path, at lower levels, would have been a delight, but altitude was beginning to exact its toll on our ability to appreciate the setting. We trekked among moss-covered boulders, lovely alpine vegetation and thrilling views. Pandim was so close that the summit could not possibly be seen without forcing the back of the head against the shoulders.

At 11 A.M. we topped out by an immense glacial erratic and promptly collapsed. Both Gillian and I could hear people talking to us, but we were not able to respond. We were sleeping as Mickey had that day when the doctors realised just how sick she really was. Kendall, Dick and Peter all insisted on rousing us until they finally succeeded in forcing some soup and tea into us. We had come as far as we could. At just under 15,000 feet, Gillian hoisted the miniature Canadian flag that had come from the cake of our farewell party a lifetime ago. With a sherpa and two porters we were sent back down to rejoin Mickey and to wait for the others. Our tents and baggage had already gone on up the mountain on the backs of the porters who seemed to thrive on the rarefied air. The others in the group would have to catch up to them at the upper camp, and send them back down to us in the late afternoon.

The trip down was much faster than the trip up. We stopped several times to force ourselves to drink, and while resting we could at least look at the moss and lichen, the alpine

First good view of Pandim - 22,500' from the trail below Dzongri at about 12000'

flowers, two different high altitude algae (one lime green, the other a deep burgundy), and assorted hardy shrubs growing bravely in the wind-shadow of a convenient rock. Our path frequently was a water course, and we simply walked on the elevated stones or the spherical clumps of what we had called, in less sensitive days, "nigger heads" in the Yukon gold fields. Some of these hummocks of grass were as big as medicine balls. Pipits flitted and did aerial acrobatics all around us, and the astounding song of a winter wren was a source of nostalgic solace.

By the time we were half-way down, the others had crossed a massive amphitheatre of a lateral morraine at the base of the Goecha La far up the valley. The smoke from their camp fire was a bitter reminder of our personal failure. They were now resting at over 16,000 feet. Gillian and I would not be sharing it with them.

What little conversation we had during the descent revolved around mountain sickness. The colour and frequency of urine were extremely important signs. The darker the colour, the more cause for alarm, and a total stoppage, of course, if prolonged would result in a backing up beyond the bladder, forcing kidney failure. Conversations like this were an added incentive to drink, drink and drink more. Overhearing the doctors, we had learned some interesting things about high altitude and its affect on the chemistry of the human body. Pain killers such as 222s become dynamite; Kendall likened them to a .22 calibre bullet. Anything with caffeine in it should be avoided, an acceptable dose at sea level being equivalent to a dozen cups of coffee at 11,000 feet. Valium and codeine are to be avoided unless as a last resort, and even then should not be used for any length of time. At altitude, the absorption rate of medicine through the mouth is critically slow. Therefore, all the main drugs on the trek are carried in injection form. This explained what Marlene Foch was referring to when she had warned us in Montreal: "Be careful, or else the doctors will stick everything into you!" All the key medication for our trek had been packed in phials, but unfortunately the pack in which they had been carried was dropped, and they all smashed. I'm glad we did not know it at the time.

Altitude sickness causes a drop-off in energy which is precipitous. By the time Gillian and I had reached camp, we were totally exhausted. The last 500 yards across the level plateau were covered in the same plodding 20 to 25 steps per minute pace that we used during the most difficult part of the journey.

We climbed into Mickey's tent, and after some forced tea we fell asleep until Norbu woke us for a refill at 6 P.M. By then, my tent had arrived with the porters who had been sent down from above. I climbed in, and drank two bowls of piping hot garlic soup for dinner. Fully clothed and hugging a hot water bottle, I slept on and off until 5:30 A.M. when I wrote in my diary:

"I haven't opened my tent flaps yet to see how October 16 – Day seven of the trek – has started. So here I am at 12,300 feet with two sick Canadians, two sherpas, six porters, and nowhere to go for another 36 hours until the rest of the party comes back. I've been in my tent, mostly sleeping, for 16 hours. When I scrunch up my lips, I can see grizzles. I haven't shaved in a week. My sinuses are screaming, and when I can finally blow my nose, the amount of blood-stained mucus is a bit unnerving. Today, if I'm up to it, and if the weather cooperates, I want to explore a cave just a couple of hundred yards from here. First, however, I have to get out of the tent. The zipper is frozen solid."

Outside, the snow, rain and sleet intermittently pelted against the tent. In the distance, the river droned just like my beloved Sainte Marguerite, but I could not convincingly imagine myself in the camp in northern Quebec where I had so often

Pandim emerging above the band
of cloud - Thangshing Camp 12,300'

fished for salmon. I made a mental note to pose for a picture in one of my Demolition Derby T-shirts with Pandim in the background, just to fill my fellow fishermen on the next D-D with seething envy. The sound could not be the Sainte Marguerite; the river, relative to my tent, was flowing in the wrong direction. So, instead of day dreaming, I tried without success to interpret the dreams of last night. Everything was disjointed. And, as my sinuses continued to drain, and the brimming tissues piled up on the tent floor I remembered that the word "mucus" seemed to have been derived from the Old Norse *myki*, meaning dung.

The dull blue womb of my tent became radiant as the sun suddenly broke over a ridge, banishing the terrible weather and thawing the zipper. Through the flap I could see the outhouse a thousand feet away. The Lomotils had been too successful, and I had been unable to get rid of any wastes for six days. This obviously had been a contributing factor to the way I had been feeling. Never has a re-balancing of the digestive track been accomplished with such a splendid view. The doors looked right up the valley past Pandim to Kangchenjunga. The river tumbled musically over its polished boulders, and six immense glossy ravens slowly glided, then hopped, then stood and then walked towards the camp. Their occasional cough seemed a fitting response to the smoke that had by now begun seeping up through the shakes in the roof of the hut. Norbu had the fire blazing, and tea was boiling.

Gillian had had a fairly acceptable night, but Mickey was doing very poorly. If she did not rally this morning, Norbu would send a sherpa back up to the next camp for one of the doctors. I felt strongly that the sherpa should be sent down to Yuksam where he could at least contact a helicopter to ferry her out. She was running a fever and had complained about a sharp pain in the chest when she breathed. Philippa

thought it might have been a pneumonic infection, which probably sounded more ominous to a layman than it really was. Gillian wrote a complete report which the sherpa would take to Bruce. By the time the sherpa arrived at the upper camp, of course, the party would have already left for the final climb to the Goecha La. Bruce and the doctors would only be able to confer late in the afternoon. We simply would have to wait.

The gloriously warm sun was short-lived. The clouds rolled up and down the valley so that we were alternately too hot and too cold. In disgust, we finally crawled back into our sleeping bags, rested and slept, and tried to regain the body fluids that we so badly needed to fight off the mountain sickness. The Dacron flaps luffed against the tent frame like a sailboat heading too high into the wind. When the sun came out, it was easy to imagine myself in St. Thomas or the Mediterranean and days spent on a warm deck, the sea breathing beneath me, and the vibrating sails painfully white against the blue sky. Can places such as those really still exist?

Twice that morning we heard the sharp reports of avalanches further up the valley. We had to assume that our trekkers were out of harm's way.

After a modest lunch, I sat around the campfire for hours, listening to Norbu tell his own story:

Norbu had had 10 years of schooling, and had spent six years teaching other teachers. He used to be "in business," carrying all manner of goods – anything that he thought might find a market – from Calcutta to Nepal, Tibet and Sikkim. His younger sister had been engaged to an American, but she had died in the same crash that claimed the life of Sir Edmund Hillary's wife. In his youth, he remembered Tenzing as the yak-herder for his mother's extensive livestock. His statement that Tenzing did not have an educated back-

ground was made factually and without the slightest trace of superiority. He also talked about the impact that Tenzing's ascent of Everest had had on the sherpa people, and had unstinting praise for all that Tenzing had done for his nation. Without deprecation he pointed out that any of many sherpas might have gone to the top, but fate decreed that Tenzing would be the first. Norbu himself had been on the mountain many times, and he was philosophical and accepting that the same fate determined that, on those days when he had been scheduled for the final assault, the weather had closed in. He mentioned the name of another sherpa who subsequently had climbed Everest six times, and his name has not become a household word, nationally or internationally.

Norbu also offered his freely given opinions on this particular trek. He stated that in his view, this was a more difficult trek than its classification would have indicated. Based on the experience of our group, he was confident that the Sikkimese tourist officials would set up way-stations at points intermediate to the established camps. He was concerned, but not unduly, about the isolation, and the fact that we would not be able to reach anyone in time for help to arrive before a minimum of three days had elapsed. In Nepal, he claimed, you could always contact someone no matter in which valley you were trekking. The lack of shoes and warm clothing among the porters was a cause of disapproval, but he did accept that the weather had been unprecedented. As I listened, I dubbined Gillian's, Mickey's and my boots, and felt as if I had put in a hard day's work. It is really sobering to see the energy of the sherpas at altitude.

An occasional sprig of rhododendron or wild herb added fragrance to the smoke, and the whole scene took on an unearthly aura. What sounded like a prolonged clap of very near thunder brought us smartly back to reality. After several seconds, Norbu and I rushed out of the hut just in time to see mammoth rocks cascading down the cliffs right behind the campsite. Great showers of sparks and billows of grey smoke wafted up from the points where the major stones collided. Then the rocks jarred to a halt, wedged among the others that had preceded them. Then, only the stream's murmuring broke the silence. Part of the path back down to civilization lies under cliffs similar to those that just spawned the rock fall. Sometimes it is better not to speculate.

The subject of yaks came up, and Norbu tried to explain that a yak is the male, a nack is the female, and that, therefore, all yak butter, rancid or not, is actually nack butter. A nack and an ox produce a *dzum*. A yak and a cow produce a *dzow*. Perhaps something was lost in translation.

About 4:15 that afternoon, Bruce and two sherpas appeared from the upper camp. Bruce gave Mickey a complete check-up and concluded she had a textbook case of acute mountain sickness. Her vital signs, however, were good, but somehow she must take in significantly greater amounts of fluids. She was basically evaporating. At 17,000 feet, the aerosol content of the air is less than one percent of that found normally at sea level. This extreme aridity causes a devastating desiccation which is aggravated with every exhalation. Your heart is working harder to do what, in the oxygen-rich atmosphere lower down, would be far from taxing. This expended energy takes its toll in perspiration. During the night, you lose fluids through breathing without replacing the lost moisture, so that by morning your raw throat gives birth to the ubiquitous "Himalayan hack." A few swallows of tea restores enough fluid to reduce the tickle, and the coughing stops.

Bruce gave Mickey a strong emetic, so something should happen. He did not feel that she would be able to move under her own steam, so he made plans to have her carried out in a makeshift litter supported by four porters. We would go with her as far as Dzongri where we would stay, but

Raven.
-
Corvus corax

she would be carried on over a "Sherpa Shortcut" directly to Bahkim where she would wait for us. There she would have a roof over her head, a bed, warmth and most importantly, she would be at 9,000 feet.

I gave the sherpas some dry socks, and, after bowls of soup, Bruce and one sherpa headed back up to base camp, fully expecting to arrive well after dark. They had started their day at 4:30 A.M. in six inches of new snow, and had climbed until 9:30, reaching 16,800 feet. None of our group, except Bruce, made it to the top of the pass, but all did go above 16,000 feet. Bruce then came back down to camp to find the message that Gillian had sent concerning Mickey, and, carrying the full 40-pound load of our portable hospital, he made it down to Thangshing in 50 minutes, an absolutely superhuman feat. He had climbed from 15,000 to 16,800 down to 12,300, and was now starting back up to 15,000 – all with a full pack, and all in one day. Bruce approached his job as group leader with total dedication. His contribution will never be forgotten by any of us who had the privilege of being on his trek.

October 17 – Day eight of the trek – Mickey had not been able to eat or drink anything last night, so physically she seemed a little weaker. She talked at length of the weird nightmares she had been having, all concerning her mother who had died 11 years ago. In one dream there were mounds of chocolate ice cream in which two pigs were wallowing. Mickey turned to her mother and demanded to know why the mother had not told her that she was as naked as a jay bird. Over to you, Sigmund.

I did not pass a good night either. It was bitterly cold, and with my sinuses in such agony I awoke every few hours to force another foul tasting swig of Tang into myself. I did feel a sense of triumph that morning to see an aspirin still perched on the rim of my Australian hat. It meant that I had taken only one pain killer during the night.

At 5:45 A.M. I could hear coughing from the girls' tent. It did not sound too good, so, after getting into my frozen boots for the fifth straight morning, I hurried over as soon as I could unzip my frozen tent. Mickey's spirits were low. She said last night that she remembered having read that there are only three reasons why someone stops eating. The first is because of the loss of a mate; the second is because of sickness; and the third is because death is imminent. She wondered out loud if she would ever again see her children. During the night there had been a lot of quite insane-sounding hooting by a tawny wood owl which reverberated up and down the valley, adding quite unnecessarily to the overall atmosphere of gloom. We hoped that the Romans had been wrong, and that there was indeed no basis for their ancient superstition about owls being harbingers of disaster.

Despite her weakness, Mickey seemed much better. Her marked improvement – she even put on make-up – may have had something to do with a remarkable occurrence of the night before, which Gillian and Norbu told me about at breakfast. Around 7 P.M., Norbu had come to Mickey's tent. He knelt over her sleeping bag while holding in his hand some raw rice, and a shallow dish of burning dried leaves and flowers spiced with rancid yak (nack) butter. He gave Mickey two grains of uncooked rice to eat. After unzipping her sleeping bag, so that her entire body was exposed (clothed) to the cold night air, he passed his hands all over her, sprinkling rice and wafting clouds of incense smoke to envelop her. All the while he muttered quiet prayers to a lama and the mountain deities. Then, very matter-of-factly, he zipped her up, and left. This morning she showed signs of energy and spirit that before had been all too lacking.

It had snowed last night, but we hoped that some sun would burn it off before the seemingly inevitable clouds started advancing up the valley by mid-morning. We were not the first to experience the frustration of this daily weather pattern. On February 28, 1881, almost exactly a century earlier, Sir Edward Temple delivered a lecture at the Evening Meeting of the Royal Geographical Society in London, entitled "The Lake Region of Sikkim, on the Frontier of Tibet." This lengthy quote brings a wry sense of déjà vu: "The bad weather we generally had was interspersed with lucid intervals of most glorious blue skies … Generally speaking, what really happened is this – early in the morning at sunrise, the weather is quite superb; the sky is unclouded azure and the mountains are unbroken white; this lasts for about three hours, that is to say, till about 10 o'clock in the day, and that is what we used to call the bloom of the morning. Then, and then only, can you take your sketches. The air is extremely cold – biting cold – and after stretching for a short time your fingers get perfectly numbed, and the only thing to do is to keep a supply of hot water close at hand, into which you can put your fingers and so get a certain amount of warmth in them, which enables you to preserve their cunning for sketching. After 10 o'clock up come the clouds. You cannot tell how they form. A little bit of vapour, no bigger than a man's hand, expands; fresh men's hands arise and clouds accumulate, till at last the whole atmosphere is clouded over. This lasts till about middle day. Then the clouds seem to turn into snow and a certain amount of snow falls in the afternoon, which makes you very miserable in the evening, and you sit down to dinner with snow all around you, and your little tent is also encrusted with snow. But towards midnight the clouds pass away, and stars come out, and it is a magnificent night. Then you have the sunrise as already described. Probably the sun when it rises will melt the thin snow during the bloom of the day."

Gillian and I had the most delicious soft-boiled eggs in the history of the universe for breakfast. Never has anything tasted so warm, soothing or right. Then tea, porridge and hot chocolate to bring up the fluid level. The fire was blazing, the porridge bubbling, and outside the sun was breaking through, just as Sir Edward had promised it would. The warmth melted the "thin snow" except in the shadow of our tents, because in shadow at high altitude the bitter cold does remain. At better than 12,000 feet, with the relatively light density of the air, the sun has few molecules on which to act. The heat of the sun that we felt was due to direct radiation. In the shade, the temperatures were markedly colder, for the surrounding air was too thin to absorb and to spread the heat. Similarly, the drop-off in temperature at day's end was remarkably fast by comparison to the change at lower levels. This same scarcity of molecules also explains why those surfaces exposed to the fire were uncomfortably hot, while our backs were actually freezing.

The hot-cold phenomenon has great repercussions on the animal, plant and insect life in the mountains. Bees that are buzzing among alpine flowers in the sun will occasionally fall to the ground absolutely comatose when the sun goes behind a thick cloud. The insects simply cannot retain sufficient heat to function. When the sun comes back out, the bees will awaken and carry on as if nothing had happened. Other insects will seek out small crevices in the rocks where some residual heat warms the trapped air, creating a highly localized micro-climate. The return of the sun brings the insects out of hiding and prompted Gillian and me to take advantage of the warmth to inspect our valley kingdom. We walked the hundred yards down to the mountain stream, and lolled on the meadow floor prodding the tiny flowers which decorated the carpets of moss. Especially beautiful were the Himalayan trumpet gentians *(Gentiana depressa).* Their deep blue tubular

blossoms dwarfed the mother plant nestled in the spongy moss. At the first drop of rain, these flowers close up tight to prevent themselves from filling up and drowning. And we saw, superimposed on the moss bed, the Himalayan edelweiss *(Leontopodium stracheyi).* Its fuzzy leaves and low profile are adaptations to protect the plant from the desiccating effects of the moisture-sparse air and the drying winds.

HIMALAYAN TRUMPET GENTIANS

The meadow was strewn with "nigger heads." Their closely matted grass-like leaves and hair-like tufts grow around a core in the most economical shape, a sphere. This combination of shape and foliage traps pockets of air, thereby creating an insulation for the root structure. In this kind of environment the plants put forth only two or three new leaves a year, and takes perhaps a decade to add one-third of an inch to its diameter. A ball a foot across will have seen the snows of a hundred winters.

Other flowers included the *Astar flaccidas,* pink with yellow centres. And in sheltered places, low bushes of miniature rhododendrons and junipers provided a surprising range of colours in their small leaves.

Because of the changes in altitude from the Gangetic Plain to the valley of Pandim, we had passed through botanical layers in a very short distance that would have required three thousand or more miles of south to north travel in Europe or North America. With the scorching temperatures at Bogdogra in the 90°F to 100°F range, and the sub-freezing temperatures on Pandim's glacial flank, and with the 123 inches of rain in Darjeeling to the frozen deserts of the Himalayan plateaus, virtually all the different climatic conditions in the world had been compressed into a vertical ascent of just under three miles. In this same cross-section of the earth are also found, therefore, representatives of the whole range of flora and fauna with only a few highly specialized exceptions.

But the plants themselves at a given altitude did not correspond exactly with those found much further north at sea level on, say, the Tundra. Although members of the same families are represented in both places, the alpine plants have had to adapt to the rarefied atmosphere with its geometrically increasing doses of radiation. As a general rule, the colours of the high altitude flowers are deeper than their low-level cousins, this being an evolutionary buffer against the ultra-violet rays. Time has been on the side of the plants. The Himalayas have been rising slowly for millennia, and are still

in the process. Without catastrophic change, the plants have had a chance to adapt to the new conditions.

The Alpine Zone is heterotropic, that is, capable of producing its own sources of organic material. In it, flowers bloom and die and revert to the nutrients that feed the next generation. Insects pollinate, birds feed on the insects (and each other), and a closed self-sustaining food chain is established. Above the Alpine Zone, however, lies the perpetual snow, totally sterile snow. Where glaciers intrude, the snow remains all year round well below the upper limits not only of the Alpine Zone but also of the forests. From where we sat, we could see plenty of bird life above the snow, and obviously they had to be feeding on something. Lawrence Swan has named this significantly different ecosystem the Aeolian Zone, after Aeolus, the mythical god of the wind.

This zone is autotropic, and depends solely on the power of the wind to blow the debris of the lower altitude systems onto the snow fields and glaciers. Millions upon millions of minute insects, dead or alive, whole or in part, from all levels – even from as far away as the Plains – and minute seeds and pollen from hundreds of miles away are deposited on the snows up to and above 20,000 feet. Insects, and in turn, the birds that feed on them, can survive therefore far above the limits of the Alpine Zone.

Cronin, in *Arun,* gives us something to ponder: on Everest, all the core samples of snow "...contained micro-organisms, proving that there is indeed some form of permanent life on the very top of the world. It seems incredible from any viewpoint and only serves to reaffirm the awesome potential of nature. In turn, man's egotism suffers another blow. He was not the first to conquer the highest summit. He was beaten there by some single-celled organisms so tiny they are hard to see with the naked eye. And while man stood but a moment on the summit before he had to rush back down to safety, these creatures call this place their home!"

Meanwhile, directly over Everest, bar-headed geese were seen flying – honking – at more than 30,000 feet. Mammals take in and expel air using the dead-ended aveoli to exchange gas. Bird lungs are relatively small, and play a secondary role in the air storage which largely takes place in an extensive air sac system. These sacs are found throughout the body wherever they can conveniently fit, and add a built-in buoyancy and lightness to the bird itself. The countless membranes in the walls of the sacs provide vast areas where oxygen exchange can take place. In addition, the breathing rate of birds is extremely high, some small passerines breathing in and out as many as 300 times per minute. The heart beats much more quickly, and the circulation of the blood is therefore correspondingly faster than in mammals. The faster the blood passes through the membranes of the lungs and air sacs the more the oxygen exchange will be enhanced. Thus, even at rarefied altitudes, levels of energy can be sustained that would be impossible for mammals. No wonder the Blyth's pipits were so effortlessly mocking our own plodding footsteps with their joyous singing and convoluted acrobatics. High above their camouflaged world, birds of prey waited for a false move.

Earlier in the trip we had seen the white-capped river chat – and we would again – at lower levels. Altitude does not bother this marvellous bird which exploits the greatest changes in height of any of the vertical migrants. It winters on the furnace-like Plain and nests up to 18,000 feet in glacial pools, feeding on insects and aquatic life, a true denizen, albeit seasonally, of the Aeolian Zone.

In contrast to the plentiful bird life, the only signs of mammals were the openings of countless burrows of the pika.

These diminutive relatives of the rabbits are very shy, preferring to go about their grass-gathering in complete privacy. Knowing they must "make hay while the sun shines," I decided to settle on the warm side of a rock and to keep watch over a likely-looking patch riddled with holes to out-wait and out-wit the rodents. Sir Edward Temple's clouds suddenly appeared out of nowhere, so the Great Pika Hunt was over. The hay is stored in chambers connected by lengthy tunnels that honey-comb the ground under and around rock piles below the frost line. As the pikas do not hibernate, their survival during the long winter depends on their industry during the summer.

The sun reappeared, and as the pikas were emerging from their hiding places, so too did Mickey emerge from her tent. The sun was wonderfully energizing. This was the first time she had been on her feet in over 60 hours. On the way back down to rejoin her, Gillian and I stopped to examine the cave we had spotted from the camp. It turned out to be a beautifully contoured overhang in a massive boulder, sculptured by water before a glacier carried the entire block to its present resting place. Under the protective ledge were the remains of a fire, and what could only be called a nest of leaves where humans had slept. The area was full of pika burrows.

This was a perfect time for a real spring cleaning of the tents. We also washed everything we could, socks, underwear and shirts, all of which dried astonishingly quickly in the arid air. The sleeping bags were given a much needed airing – we had been sleeping in the same clothes for over a week.

Domestic chores out of the way, we took advantage of the prolonged sunny spell to walk back with Mickey to the mountain stream. There were gentians dotting the moss, stag horn lichen, wintergreen berries and small red and mauve blossoms on the bushes. A bleached yak bone was the perfect prop for a photograph of "Mickey's first meal," dubbed predictably, her "Big Yak Attack." Everything seems funnier at 13,000 feet.

The walk felt wonderful, but it confirmed that Mickey was nowhere nearly ready to do much without help. She had to be helped back to the tent where Norbu was waiting with hot tea. As the girls rested, I read them selected passages from *Shibumi*. As any unacclimatized trekker will confirm, the Delights of the Razor described in the book totally, completely lose their edge at 13,000 feet.

By 11 A.M. the first two porters from the upper camp had come down. No doctors, Daku or Bruce, so we assumed they felt confident that Mickey was past the danger point. She was able to stand the smoke of the hut for lunch, and relished the last egg. Norbu looked resplendent in his green Swiss tuque on which Gill had sewn a small Canadian flag. I dubbined the boots again.

Starting around 1:15, one by one the other sherpas and porters began trickling in, and they were sincerely delighted that we, especially Mickey, were feeling better. By 1:45 the camp was fog-bound. The others would have to grope their way down. The first of the stragglers were Greg and Daku, as we had all expected. Daku was not the least surprised that Mickey was much improved because the porter had told her that Mickey had undergone the rice treatment. "I promise she will be all right," he had said. "If not, you can do anything you want to with me." In time, Peter, Kendall, Dick and Philippa came in. Philippa's reaction was most interesting: she urged Mickey to have a second incantation rather than take more western medicine. And that is what she did.

At 4:15 the real shaman, along with Norbu, Sonam, the egg man and the other lead sherpas and porters came to the tent where the three of us were huddled against the cold.

A dish of charcoal incense was set beside the flap, and a balming smoke wafted in while the shaman, squatting under his fleece tunic, intoned several minutes of prayers and chants. He then sucked in sharply and spat out twice, then twice more, offering Mickey three grains of rice. Then, with the sickness transmitted into the old rice, he threw the bad grains away, and added lumps of butter to the smouldering incense, thus changing the properties of the smoke.

Prior to all this, I had had a very severe sinus attack. With perhaps five inhalations of the medicinal smoke I could feel everything in my head drain, dry and clear. I wanted to breathe in more, but could only wait on the periphery of the cure that was intended for someone else. The shoes of the miracle workers were now on the other feet.

It was like a homecoming to have everyone back together again for supper. We sat around the fire discussing a myriad of things, and the three Canadians listened with envy to the descriptions of the sights we had missed. Dick had fallen into a glacial pool and was very fortunate not to have suffered frost bite or worse. With his bad hip, he was lucky to be able to clamber back onto dry land.

Then back under moonlit clouds to our tents. Dick had turned in early, and the strains of a Mozart violin concerto competed gently with the snow waters which called to each other from their rivulets. Soon, night frost would hush their voices under an etched canopy of ice. In the morning, the sun would again loose their tongues; and murmuring, then babbling, then joyously shouting they would carry their natal hill, speck by suspended speck, to the stream, to the torrent, to the river to the Plain. Their gift from the hills would bring crops to men who would never set eyes on these peaks, but who would be grateful.

Tomorrow, we start home. We shall never see our valley or Pandim again, but they will always be with us.

Griffon Vulture

89

October 18 – Day nine of the trek – Another hard frost, but despite waking up after each half-hour dream, I got through the night without having to take a single aspirin. And, *mirabile dictu,* my nasals did not start to drip at first light. The incense had helped more than the Contact-C!

At 5:15 Sonam and the other sherpas sang their way through camp, bringing washing water and morning tea. Mickey's headache was back. Bruce had hoped that she would have been able to walk out, at least part way, but it now looked as if she would have to be carried. The day would probably be very bad. It was cloudy and cold, and there was bound to be snow in the passes and pastures above Dzongri. Even before negotiating that segment, Mickey would have to climb down about 2000 feet through the boulders to the river, then back up to over 15,000 feet to skirt the camp, thus shortening the time required to reach the lower altitudes. We knew that it had snowed each of the past five mornings, but there was no way of telling how much melting had taken place during the day. Even the lower sections might be miserable. At least every step would be one step closer to getting back to safety.

At 6:00 A.M., Mickey, looking very puffy, ate two soft boiled eggs. This frugal meal could not have been further from the obsessive dreams we had been having about food of late. The "dream meal" that kept haunting me was the one I had had in 1959 at Cap Rousse in Corsica: pâté de merle, grilled spiny lobsters with cream cognac sauce, and a chilled chablis. The only impurity was the dessert – chocolate ice-cream – something we all craved.

At 6:15, dressed in her warmest clothes, Mickey started off on her own two feet down the trail behind the smoking hut. We all stood and applauded. She lasted less than 25 yards. She would have to be carried.

Norbu and the porters fashioned a harness out of a sleeping mat, which they wrapped in a figure-eight around the porter and Mickey's posterior. Then they hoisted her – all five-feet six inches of her – onto the back of a porter who could not have been four-feet eleven inches. With her knees tucked up to keep her feet from dragging, she completely covered the porter's back, obstructing any sight of him other than the bulging calves of his legs. After a false start, he stopped, and incredibly, removed his shoes. Then the evacuation team headed off down the trail at a speed beyond anything we could match. Within minutes, a giant boulder intervened, and they were lost of view.

It seems appropriate to insert here Mickey's own unedited words, written after she had reached Bahkim, where she would wait for the rest of us to catch up.

~

October 16th – The last two days for me are almost blank; just faint blurs of reality – thinking and experiencing so many feelings – wanting to die, almost – nausea with every smell – a head which will burst any minute – desperation: "not another exhortation to swallow, please!" Impossible, and yet they tell me it's their only answer. To put my head down and sleep is my only answer. Strange, no matter what the result? Doctors hovering around, all having different opinions – pills – hours – so many times, what does it matter. Go! I'm not worried – I can't think – I'm burning up – pain – pain – just go! Yes, Norbu will stay – The day goes by – delirious and dreaming, with everything floating deliciously. Strange dreams of dead people: some funny and others dreary – Please don't wake – someone unzips my sleeping bag and two grains of rice are put into my mouth for me to eat – the smell of incense and the sound of chanting invades my tent – beads and more rice are sprinkled over me – at last: sleep drifts in and there is nothing – *October 18th* (on arrival at Bahkim) – I sit huddled in my penthouse room, wearing all the clothes I brought plus a sleeping bag to cuddle me as much as possible, after I have gently affirmed to Norbu that this is my own room and that he should move all his gear into any other room. The view is not a new one for me, of course, but now, I have the luxury of the realisation that I can view the likes of these tops and valleys quietly from my bed because I have actually survived my trip here. Let me regress a bit – when I awoke this A.M., not feeling well at all after a night and two days of headaches, nightmares and creeping edema, it was decided that I would be carried down with three porters and one sherpa – I started very bravely after tearful farewells from Gillian and David, for I would not be seeing them for two days – I would be brought to a much lower level. And so we started our descent. I walked for 20 minutes (here, she meant yards) but at a pace that no one could stand and so the first porter took over. A sling was produced – it is made of sturdy rope. A large towel is also produced (actually, it was a sleeping mat) and it fits under my ass and over his forehead (I sit piggy-back). I'm told to hold my legs as high as possible. The first part of my journey is across large boulders and many rivers, always climbing, and I'm lurched forward. And, surprisingly after holding my breath in sheer panic for a few seconds, I realise that the porter is extremely sure-footed – but *bare*-foot. We move on at a terrific pace, in and out of snow; paths laden with chopped or fallen rhododendron trees, my face is nestled in his neck – I am completely at the mercy of his expertise.

I start to think back that three days ago the smoky hashish-like smells from the porters were making me ill. And now these very same smells are in the process of becoming part of my own body – Because of the porter's sinewy and light body structure, his every laboured movement is felt and transmitted onto my breast and chest bones in a way that the

pain makes us cooperative partners in his struggle. Sweat has now permeated all of my front (three layers) and the rope pulls at my crotch and I pray that he wants to stop for a real rest (not just the slowing down marked by a long whistle). The idiocy of my thought alone angers me – so difficult for such a short man to manoeuvre one with such long legs laden with heavy hiking boots.

But soon we all rest – we're in the snow now and it is *very* cold, Daku has now reached us and later on Greg – a few jokes, a few joints among the porters (I think maybe being stoned is the only way they can do their work!). Scratch that out please! Time for the other porter – he's the young, handsome one – again the same thing happens, and I look down to see that he's wearing rubbers full of holes and two sizes too large. We relentlessly continue downwards into a ravine from an elevated ridge 13,600 feet – Norbu uses his ice pick to determine the depth of snow and its stability, sometimes carving steps while my porter tries to find a footing – this is called a "Sherpa Short-cut." The front of me is again permeated with his sweat but the rest of me is freezing – he has a habit of spitting regularly and sometimes part of the spittle greets my hand. The rope is pulling me apart and I feel the breast bone pain again – He slips and blessedly we fall backwards – giggles! Thank God. The ridge is narrow and we reach the mud – slipping quite frequently; but I never fear for my safety – I know his every reaction by now and marvel at his stamina. When we reach the short cut trail to Bahkim we part from Daku, her sherpas and porters – she must go on to Dzongri – the view we have is magnificent. I have never seen this part before – valleys and glaciers being revealed by floating clouds at my feet – sometimes a royal blue sky as a background for shiny silver peaks. All is too much for the eye to take in – especially when my head is meant to be as low as possible to help the porter's equilibrium. They then permit me to walk a while – but again I am too slow. It is decided that speed is of the essence. In sherpa language that means: run down the hills, cliffs, rocks, waterfalls. The shoeless porter begins at a pace that is used in dog races. I am mesmerized as I see the mud oozing between his toes and watch in fascination those toes grip like suction cups on these greasy rocks – the path is narrow and tortuous as he twists and turns at right angles teetering over thousands of feet of sheer drop, never varying the speed, much as an amusement park car manoeuvers its turns as if attached mechanically to its track. This man, however, is not computerized and I blank out all thoughts of a mis-step! I concentrate instead on the beautiful and exquisite mosses of yellow, pinks and bright greens, all hiding their treasured berries of electric blues and reds.

At last we arrive – a room overlooking the world! A shelter at 9,000 feet. It is 5:30 P.M., almost dark. I still possess half a candle for light and what remains of a weak beam of light from a disposable torch (flashlight). The kitchen in the shelter, it would seem, is not open – so Norbu decides to prepare the dinner of my choice in the "other kitchen" which is in a farm hut down the path. I'm summoned to dinner at six – Thank God – (because I'm trying to save my candle) and I'm tired of lying here in the dark – We arrive at a "Tibetan refugee" household for dinner – however, we must pass through the shed where the meat is being dried and hung – a process which gives off its own decaying odours which are shared with the garbage heap. The floor is mud and the animals move about freely. We enter the "kitchen" very dimly lit by three kerosene lamps (the kind with only a wick). The hearth stone is in the centre of focus with a long rhododendron branch stuck in the front through a primitive hole near the floor – on either side are the cinders which mercifully will keep warm the fluffy rice already cooked. Several tea pots and other black encrusted pots stand on the top receiving the full results of a forever-stoked stove – smoke of course covers the greater part of the upper ceiling, but surprisingly, I can see without tears or wincing. The grandmother looking all or more of her 65 years (we saw her on the road to Dzongri) holding a very cherubic rosy-cheeked child on her lap while stroking another in what I would qualify as a litter box. Father (the handsome tall man we also saw on the road selling eggs) is also next to the stove standing with his Scottish cap on, churning his yak butter, the mother fully laden with Tibetan silver jewelry which I eye with envy, is busily putting the finishing touches to the dinner and to yesterday's butter which she molds and makes disappear as quickly as her filthy feet will take her.

It is much later in my room now: candlelight reveals large shadows of me in the shelter, alone – echoes of my own slow footsteps in the cold dank halls open to the exterior. There is a Sikkimese bat in my room. At first I'm terrified but I keep the candle on because I must finish writing this. Too early to sleep – too cold – too lonely but somehow I am not frightened at 9,000 feet alone in the Himalayas – how strange! This bat keeps on buzzing me and I can't stand it anymore – blow the candle – try to sleep – take pills – can't swallow it, water makes me gag – darkness. I hear the bat squeaking and scratching – I hear a horse and a goat down the path, reassuring sounds – sleep – I think of holding my children to me.

Sunday – *October 19th* – I feel better today – no sunrise over the glaciers. No, just damned clouds. I'm depressed and dreary – can't wait to see the ones I love. My sleeping bag is cold – shake out the boots before putting them on. Put down jacket on but no balaclava today (first time I've worn no hat in five days). I hate going to the bathroom – so cold – try to wash a bit – icy water – Norbu promises to warm it for me and makes breakfast at the neighbours'. Same entrance only now in daylight I see the carcasses of meat spread out like kites in the ceiling and garbage piles in the corner – stench – chickens all around – the kitchen is clean now and the children are around me while I force down two eggs: all I've had in five days – a few biscuits and Tibetan yak tea (terrible salty taste). Grandmother, very attentive, brings me rugs in hope that I will buy. Father proudly displays knives with same thought in mind – the smoke begins to fill my lungs again – I must get out for air.

I still feel ill, but it is time for exercise. Norbu forces me to walk up steep hills to strengthen my legs. There will be time for rest later for I must be ready to meet Gillian and David, whom I missed enormously, and continue to trek with all the others and make my way back to my home and all the loved ones I left behind.

~

Meanwhile, back up at Thangshing, the rest of us started down, leaping across swollen sheets of melt water, picking our way through boulders and carefully hopping from hummock to hummock. But at least we were heading down! The sun was warm by the time we had crossed the river at that wonderfully beautiful spot where we had had such a treasured lunch. It seemed so long ago. Then it was back up the steep forest trail, up towards hated/beloved Dzongri; hated, because it was so high, so far, so cold, so uncomfortable; beloved, because from there on it would be almost all down hill. And, who could tell, perhaps we might see the fabled view.

The trek up the valley wall was an extravaganza of beauty. The sun was out, and the peaks we had not seen originally were thrusting against the sky as far as we could see. We tried to match the giants with the indications on the map, and we think we saw Jhopunu (pronounced "Jannu") at

19,470 feet, Arrlungtsur at 15,500 feet, and of course, beloved Pandim standing guard at the entrance to the valley leading to Kangchenjunga. It was as if we were walking across giant pages of a geology text book, a vista so broad, so overwhelmingly spectacular that no film could really do it justice. The sounds and the air, the sun, the tightness of our muscles, our short breathing – all these gave a tactile, sensory element that by necessity eludes the camera.

After about an hour, we rounded a spur, and left Pandim and her neighbours behind, only to come upon an even more spectacular – if that was possible – barricade of huge peaks. I chose a dry spot to sit (and rest) so that I could try a quick sketch while my fingers retained "their cunning." The sun would not wait for me, and each moment brought new features into focus, obliterating others. The field sketch succeeded in capturing a sense of immediacy, but the detail was highly arbitrary. I resorted to my Ashai Pentax for overlapping panoramic shots, and it was on these that my final drawing was based.

Interestingly, despite the overwhelming scenery, the attention of most of the members of the group was riveted to the miniaturized beauty that encircled us on this part of the trail. Droplets of water coated all the hanging mosses and infused the leaf surfaces with a million prisms of fire. These natural gems surpassed anything crafted by man. Ah! de Beers, where now is thy sting?

The path kept climbing up, up to about 14,400 feet, through soggy snow fields with millions of rhododenrons silhouetted against the whiteness like so many chevrons or helicopter blades. Then the inevitable and all pervading dampness rolled in to envelop us completely. Gillian was in frightful shape with a mega-migraine. We stopped every half hour to force more liquids into our resisting bodies, and we searched for trail marks through the slush and the omnivorous fog. On the rounded shoulder of a snow-covered peak we could see the trail that Mickey and the porters must have taken. Lest we follow the same route, our sherpas had marked an arrow in the snow with a ski pole. As I write this, it suddenly occurs to me that nowhere have I mentioned the fact that we used a ski pole to add balance and to give extra lift throughout the trek. This proved to be of great help. All I wanted was to reach Dzongri so that I could rest and warm up. Others, however, were in much better shape, for they launched off on mini-excursions to the left and right of the trail to investigate some isolated chortons. At varying times, therefore, the group straggled into camp. It was still ghastly weather, and there was not a hint of the Dzongri view.

During the trek, I had been keeping my copious notes in a steno pad, and whenever I felt inspired, I would add a sketch. The porters and the sherpas had not let this go unnoticed, and now a group of them confronted me as I was sitting on a stone outside the smoky confines of the Dzongri hut bringing my diary up-to-date. They were fascinated by the "magic pen," and wanted me to draw a portrait. I tried to satisfy their curiosity by showing them the various drawings that I had already done, but as they identified each with appreciative clucks and twitters, their keenness to have me do something for them just grew. The greatest temptation was for me to draw their marvellous faces and caps and boots, but I really hesitated to try it. The two most obvious problems were the finite limits to my talent, and secondly, the conditions could not have been worse. I was frozen and so was my pen. But the third reason was the one that really worried me. For whatever reasons, they expected a lot of me, and if I failed to create a likeness that matched their anticipation, they would not only have been disappointed, but they also might have been offended, thinking so inaccurately that I had drawn them in a way that was insulting. I also thought of

the two yak women on the trail who were obviously terribly
concerned about the evil eye of the camera. They would
not let us take pictures. Sketching the sherpas and porters
was not, therefore, something to be taken lightly. Nevertheless,
they insisted. Without a doubt, one of the most fascinating
faces belonged to our number two sherpa, Sonam. Shyly, he
posed while I sat on an icy plank next to a yak yurt. His
face was remarkably broad, and I had to keep adding width
to his felt hat to accommodate the expanse of his forehead. The
result was unmistakably Sonam, and sure enough, all the
others wanted their portraits done as well. Playing for time, I
promised them the moon, but first had to do a detailed
study of a great pair of sherpa boots. I was spared the portrait
session by the welcomed call for lunch. And the scheduled
sitting after lunch was permanently delayed by the arrival of
seven *dzums*, absolutely laden down with duffles and food.
These shaggy beasts emerged from the fog, announced by the
muffled tinkling of bells. Rumours had preceded them that
a group of French trekkers was heading our way. As we had
already set up our tents in the only available space, this
invasion might cause some problems.

Our "French" turned out to be 11 trekkers, several of whom
were from Geneva, a Swede from Gothenberg, a girl from
Rimouski, Quebec, and a handful of Parisians under the
leadership of a member of the Jacquot family of Chamonix.
They were all very grateful for the use of our fire and biscuits, and in exchange they told us the gold fixing of eight
days previously, that the U.S. Grand Prix had been won
by Jones, and that Iran was attacking Bagdad and Iraq was
attacking Teheran. They had seen Mickey being carried out,
and one Frenchman, to the resigned disgust of his wife,
repeated again and again: "C'était une femme magnifique!"

The fog invaded the hut, and with the *dzums* stumbling
around outside the door, the atmosphere was unearthly. I spent

The sound of Sonam's cheerful voice
every morning - "More-neeng! Hod tea -
washywadder, More-neeng!" - will
forever be a vivid part of the memories
of this trip.

the afternoon listening enthralled as Dick described the evolution of plastic surgery, and the kinds of reconstructive operations that were his specialty. The gory details did nothing to lessen the appetite, and by the time supper was ready, so were we. Excellent chicken soup, followed by pan-fried beans and carrots, a basketball-sized boiled cabbage stuffed with a tuber of ginger, roast chickens, with exotic fruit salad and thick cream for dessert. I think the kitchen staff was trying to impress the newcomers from France.

By 8:30 we headed back through the snow to our tents. Dick's Mozart and the animated conversation of the French group lulled me to sleep, feeling sea level fine for the first time. I awoke, totally refreshed and raring to go at 11 P.M.! From then on, I awoke every hour on the hour, but put the time to profitable use by dreaming of tomorrow when we would climb a little, then straight down 4000 feet to Bahkim. From there, it would be a half day to Yuksam and the waiting jeeps. I was suffering now from a nostalgic case of "channel fever," something I last felt as the *S.S. Gander Bay* slipped up the glycerin smooth St. Lawrence River on the way home to Montreal after a summer of incredible experiences in the eastern Canadian arctic. I could hardly contain myself. The anticipation of home was nerve-wracking. After a quarter of a century, the feeling was the same.

October 19 – Day ten of the trek – We awoke to the song of Sonam, yak bells and the noises of the other tents at 5:30. We exchanged pleasantries with the Franco-Swiss group who had interspersed their tents with ours, and whose unfamiliar voices – no, more the unfamiliar cadence of their voices – inspired a twing of jealousy. This was our Dzongri, not theirs. Over breakfast, we learned that they did not have a doctor with them, that virtually everything would be carried on the backs of their *dzums* and yaks, each of which, they claimed, replaced a minimum of four porters. They all seemed woefully under-equipped, and a little too trusting in blind faith. It also struck us that every last one of them smoked continuously. But then again, so did all our porters. Not one of our group smoked.

Ours would be a short day, and so we were in no great rush to start off. The other group headed up into the fog and snow, animals lurching, with lots of Gallic animation. By 8:30 A.M. the clouds had lifted enough to form a ceiling over the valley at just our eye level. Below the cloud, everything was in sharp detail; above, we could not see a thing. Somewhere out there was the fabled view of the 20,000 foot peaks in Nepal, and one of the unforgettable sights of Kangchenjunga. Then again, the tourist brochure claimed that we should at that moment be standing ankle-deep in glorious wild flowers rather than shin-deep in slush.

"After breakfast we bid a not-too-fond farewell to Dzongri, and climbed a thousand feet to the edge of a ravine. Suddenly exploding from a rhododendron forest was a male Impeyan pheasant – peacock iridescent with a rufous tan tail. It flew by me at about 50 feet before collapsing into the forest."

That laconic entry in my diary hardly did justice to the most exciting ornithological moment of the entire trip. In fact, when I saw the Impeyan or Monal (or Daphne or nine-coloured pheasant of Nepal) pheasant, I began screaming like a man possessed, which indeed I was. For I had just seen a bird which others have called thus: "this singularly beautiful species" (John Latham, *A General History of Birds,* 1822); "all is resplendent" and "a splendid bird" (John Gould, *A Century of Birds of the Himalayas,* 1832); "the splendor and changeability of the tints upon the male of this bird, it is almost impossible to describe either by words or the pencil" (Sir William Jardine, *Naturalist's Library,* 1834); "entitled to carry off the palm for beauty" (Daniel Giraud Elliot, *A Monograph of the Phasianidaie,* 1872); "quite unsurpassed for

Himalayan Monal or Impeyan Pheasant
Lophophorus impeyanus

splendor" (Richard Lydekker, *The Royal Natural History,* 1895). Lydekker added a quote from a Mr. Hume, who described the bird "shooting horizontally out just below, glittering, flashing like a gigantic rainbow tinted gem, and then dropping stone-like with closed wings into the abyss below." Obviously, Mr. Hume had been standing a century ago at the exact same spot!

In describing the bird, Gould's words frankly failed him. Elliot had better luck, and is worthy of being quoted at length:

"Head, throat, and fore-part of the neck covered with pointed scale-like feathers, metallic green, with blue reflections; a long crest, having the shafts bare of webs unto their tips, where are spatules of metallic green. Back and sides of neck fiery red, exceedingly brilliant in the sunlight. Mantle metallic green, with the edges of feathers in certain lights red. Wings rich purple, the feathers tipped with changeable blue and green. Secondaries purplish brown, the edges metallic green. Primaries dark brown. Middle of the back white. Upper tail-coverts purple, like the wings, tipped with green. Entire underparts black; a line of feathers running along the sides of the neck brilliant green. Under tail-coverts black, tipped with green. Tail rich tan colour. Bill black. Feet and tarsi dark brown...Naked skin of face restricted blue."

If words were inadequate, so too was the full page hand-coloured lithograph by Elizabeth Gould in her husband's great *Century of Birds,* a picture re-copied in miniature by Jardine for his hand-coloured copper engraving in the *Naturalist's Library* volume on gallinaceous birds in which he called the Gould portrait "by far the best which have ever appeared of this" species. Up to that time, the "best" had been none too good. In 1822 a quarto hand-coloured engraving appeared in Latham's *A General History of Birds* which looked as if an appallingly badly stuffed pheasant had just stuck its

beak into an anachronistic electrical outlet. The first portrait to begin to do justice to the bird was one of the masterpieces in animal art, painted by Joseph Wolf, and transferred onto stone and coloured by John Keulemans for Elliot's *Phasianidae* in 1872. For those who are familiar with Wolf and Keulemans, it will come as little surprise that Elliot's monograph has been acclaimed the most beautiful bird book of all time. The plate of the Impeyan pheasant is one of the most beautiful.

Lady Impey, the wife of the first British Governor-General of Bengal, pioneered the keeping and raising in captivity of this marvellous creature. In the early 1810s she sent some to England. To quote Latham: "Lady Impey attempted, with great prospect of success, to bring some of them to England, but after being on board for two months they caught a disorder from other poultry and died." It was in her honour that the birds were named, and it was the skins that so overwhelmed the illustrators and lovers of natural history of the period.

The first successful hatching and rearing in Europe was at the London Zoo and the Jardin d'Acclimatation in Paris in 1854 and 1856. In 1832, Gould had predicted "if introduced into our country (they) would form a splendid ornament to our woods and lawns." Bird dealers took up the challenge and supplemented the European-bred stock with imports. Between 1864 and 1882, more than 2000 Impeyans (and Satyr tragopans) were brought from India to England, and as many as 50 a year were exported from Calcutta every spring from 1922 to 1940 when the war interrupted the trade.

Birds this beautiful would be doomed unless they had something more than isolation to protect them. In the 1880s a Colonel Tickell said their taste reminded him of peafowl, "but no part being fit for anything but soup in old specimens."

According to modern books, the Impeyan pheasant frequents open forests particularly of oak, birch and rhododendron

100

with open glades and grassy slopes from about 6,000 feet up to the snow line between 12,000 and 13,000 feet. As interesting as that fact may be, the anthropomorphism of a century and a half ago is a lot more fun; in the 1829 edition of Cuvier's *Animal Kingdom,* the translator revealed that "it delights in lofty mountains and solitary wilds." And Jardine recognized that it "enlivens these stupendous solitudes."

We walked seemingly forever, back up to 14,500 feet, through more snow and slush, then mercifully started down through the flat field where we had camped at Lower Dzongri. A lot of snow had fallen, and the rhododendrons were all hinged downwards. But the sun and the drop in altitude had the irresistible effect of bringing us back to the tropics, because–it was easy to forget–that is where we really were.

It was as if I had never been on this trail before. The mosses, lianas, berries, fungus and flowers were all new. Most arresting of all, however, were tiny "hoodoos." Small pebbles against exposed banks or cuts protected the earth immediately below them as would an umbrella. Erosion took its toll all around, but left the pebble standing on top of the column of dirt that it was shielding. Many of the columns were several inches high, miniaturized versions of the same geological formations in the badlands of the Canadian west where the pebbles are monster boulders, and the columns are hundreds of feet high. This particular stretch of the trail consumed two rolls of film–and not one picture of a mountain.

Late in the morning we passed through Tzokha, the Tibetan refugee village, now the first, not the last outpost of civilization. The fog had by now rolled in and was swirling around the clutter of the wooden huts, and probing every nook and cranny for a chance to add an air of mystery. Man was doing his own bit to achieve an unreal atmosphere. From one of the buildings emanated the doleful repetition of a gong

being struck, no doubt with the thigh bone of a deceased monk. Chants and incantations and the occasional blast of a horn added counterpoint. Everything else was completely muffled by the fog.

As it turned out, one particularly modest hovel was the home of Sonam's mother and siblings. We were invited in for a cup of tea, laced heavily with yak butter. Had one been weaned on this rancid brew, our own tea would appear insipidly bland. One swallow was more than enough. Politeness, however, dictated that we receive with thanks her proffered hospitality. It was her way of thanking the group for the medical miracle that had just befallen her. Dick, after many years of the bloodiest kind of medicine, described it as unlike anything he had ever encountered. Sonam had asked him to see his mother who had, he feared, an ulcerated leg. With appropriate demureness, the old woman removed her undergarments, letting loose a stench that defied description. On the upper thigh there was a clearly defined hole about the size of a quarter, and quite deep. The exposed flesh at the bottom of the crater looked suspiciously rosy and firm. A smart tap at the rim dislodged a chunk of filth. The ulcer was not in the leg, it was in the dirt. She had not washed in her entire adulthood. Her leg had become completely encrusted in a layer of mud. Outside, ravens and jungle crows sat on the dead malevolent fingers of fog-shrouded trees, and croaked.

Lower down in the cloud forest we rested in a glade, and after sitting as still as the beads of perspiration and the dripping condensation from the canopy would allow, we attracted assorted white-cheeked bulbuls, crested tits, alpine robin accentors, and a scaley wren babbler that I thought was a drab coloured pita. A flock of laughing thrushes was in hysterics. There were hundreds of birds flitting just too fast and too far away to be identified, but evident enough to confirm that a trek devoted to birding would not be in vain.

Besides the Impeyan pheasant, the nicest thing that happened today was having the loop on my plastic water bottle break. How I had come to loath it! I gave it to Sonam's mother. Unencumbered by its constant banging against my back, my pace quickened, and by noon I was taking my own sherpa shortcuts, and was in Bahkim. Mickey was waiting, and looking absolutely fine. Now back at 9,000 feet, our appetites returned, and we wolfed down four heaping helpings of curried cabbage with melted cheese, pears and lots of tea. Even our muscles felt better. Going up is considerably easier than coming down, but in either direction each trekker is far better off to set his or her own pace. To speed up or to slow down to accommodate someone else is an investment in sociability that pays dividends in exhaustion and aching limbs.

We spent the afternoon bundled up in wicker chairs on the terrace watching the cold clouds insinuate themselves into everything. Way in the distance, we could see houses in the sun where people were actually warm. Some of us wrote in our diaries, others rested, and still others tried to identify bushes full of confusing leaf warblers. The *Phylloscopus* genus is a nightmare, posing perhaps the toughest field identification problem in all birddom. They are all dull green above, paler below. In this case, a bird in the hand is worth about 15 in the field guide, especially when the local plates hardly match those of a Roger Tory Peterson. When asked what a particular bird might be, our resident birder, Nemesis, rather haughtily apologized for not knowing the names in English, she only knew them as *Phylloscopus*. Kendall, at that point, excitedly asked to borrow my binoculars. Focusing on a non-existent bird in a tree, his exclamations of awe prompted Nemesis to ask what it was that he saw. "I'm afraid I don't know the English name," he deadpanned, "but in Latin its *Nemesis vulgaris vulgaris.*"

Scampering under the windows was the Himalayan squirrel, in all probability the same one we had seen on the way up. At that time it had not seemed very special; this time it did, for during the entire trek through the forest this turned out to be the only ground level animal that we saw. Down in the valleys we had seen and would again see troops of rhesus monkeys, and above the tree line we had seen a small member of the weasel family. But in the forest itself we had seen nothing. Snapping twigs and heavy crashing through the undergrowth indicated that animals were present, and later on, pelts of the red panda hung on the door at Tenzing's home would confirm that mammals do exist where we walked. Contrary to the image presented by jungle movies, the rain forest does not abound in readily visible animal life. In fact, the rain forest does not provide a habitat conducive to concentrations of mammals, nor does it offer environmental niches to be filled by a spectacular diversity of forms. The greatest number and variety of mammals are found either in the grasslands or the drier forests. Where these two habitats interface with the rain forest there is an artificial concentration of wildlife that belies the reality of what is to be found in the zone of perpetual moisture and sullen light. In the understory, insects, birds, some bats and invertebrates such as the delightful leeches represent the most obvious forms of life. It is in the canopy that major mammal concentrations live their lives usually hidden from view from the trekkers below. We had seen troops of langurs hurtling through the canopy at astounding speeds, and had been the recipients of their shrieks and howls as well as being pelted by them with fruits and large fleshy-husked nuts.

We spent part of the afternoon playing frisbee with two little girls who were more like animals than humans. They bit, scratched, hit, kicked and threw things at each other with intent to hurt, and with no sign of remorse. It must be very difficult to learn social graces in an isolated environment such as this.

By this time, I had become chilled to the bone, and felt as badly as I had at any time during the entire trip. Finally, at supper, Daku gave me a hot water bottle which I tucked up under my down-filled jacket, and this helped cure the involuntary shivers.

This is the first night under a roof since we were last in this same spot. We would never have to sleep in our tents again. I would never have to drink out of that cursed plastic bottle, and I swore that I would frisbee the next ice-cold tin dinner plate.

October 20 – Day eleven of the trek – Our last day of trekking! This has come none too soon. And it has started off typically – it rained all night, and the clouds this morning are tiered high above and far below. The various spurs rise out of the fog like islands. All this moisture means "very leeches," as Daku would say. The little devils will have one last crack at me after all.

We came down through breathtaking scenery in the cloud forest, this time completely enveloped with steam. Overhead, troops of langurs screeched and hurled rotten fruit, leeches jumped out from the overhanging leaves, and a yak train overtook us. Wind eddies would thin the clouds and suddenly the sound of a waterfall would take on a ribbon of plunging white. All shades were muted greys and greens, with an occasional explosion of brilliant red or yellow where a large blossom beckoned the twittering birds. Four-foot palmated leaves of a relative of the monstera plant were glazed in glycerin-like moisture, moss completely covered rock and fallen tree alike. And our path was strewn with small purple and tiny yellow orchids.

We crossed a wooden bridge which spanned a torrent that drained the clouds above, only to disappear into the ferns

Yak train – Bahkim / Yuksam trail

below, pausing on its relentless journey to scour a sculptured pool in which two plubeous redstarts held sway. When not hopping wag-tail-like over the slippery rocks, they would dart out to hover hummingbird-like before some tubular orange flowers. Mickey rested here while Norbu patiently allowed a monster leech to inch along his bare hand so that I could take a close-up photo.

Beyond the bridge, the trail headed steeply up for one last gasp. Suddenly, through a break in the jungle and a break in the clouds, we could see Yuksam, still two hours away, but nevertheless within sight. It was a powerful impact. The fog coalesced around us, and we had to put our rainwear over us despite the fact that it was not raining.

The trail became wider, and the mud was imprinted with many more footsteps than our group could have caused. The jungle gave way to fields and stone walls, and the silence was finally broken by the sound of bells and the exhortations of a farmer coaxing his yoke of oxen through a reluctant pasture of stones where his wooden plow turned a primitive furrow. How could our world, our priorities, even our century have any meaning for him?

And finally Yuksam, with its neat compound of pale yellow, red-roofed buildings, riotous flowers, marigolds against cut stone walls, exquisite mauve orchids, and a welcoming flock of tree sparrows. I could not believe it was over. In my diary I wrote: "Now may the human anesthesia blot out the pain, the nausea, the hurting, and let the incredible – truly incredible – memories take full possession."

During lunch we listened to five large roosters reluctantly becoming part of the preparations for our dinner. In our supermarket society we tend to forget that heads have to be lopped off, and that boiling water singes feathers out by the handful.

And we shed our excess impediments. I gave my other hated water bottle to Norbu, and disposed of socks, T-shirts and long-johns. The sherpas would be able to make better use of them than I would. We also gave away all leftover dehydrated fruits and vegetables, fruit crystals, quick energy mixtures of chocolate, nuts and raisins and a packet of freeze-dried chocolate ice-cream. These, and extra rolls of toilet paper would come in handy for those of the group who would be heading on to Bhutan. Our "deaccessorizing" was interrupted by Sonam's call for an old fashioned English high tea, complete with an immense cake that had been baked in a iron pot, into which a lining of sand had been poured around a smaller pot, in which the cake itself was done to perfection over the glowing coals that had been banked around and on top of the Himalayan version of a Dutch oven. Small sandwiches, muffins and pots of steaming tea were almost too incongruous. The rest of the afternoon was devoted entirely to sloth and indolence.

Sections of giant bamboo, more than a foot high and a good six inches across, were filled with a combination of various fermenting grains and very hot water. We toasted friendship and safe return with these rustic tankards of tomba, the wonderfully potent native drink. Then dinner was served: deep-fried whole potatoes with soya sauce, pan stirred carrots, and our reluctant chickens roasted to a tender crispness. Then, with the dishes cleared away, our mess hall became a theatre for the local young students who had arrived in native dress to interpret for us their Tibetan and Sikkimese songs and dances. Their orchestra consisted of a drummer and a cymbal player. Norbu acted as the master of ceremonies, and introduced each dance with a laboured explanation that invariably brought shouts of laughter from the sherpas who understood both the original and the attempted translation. The dancing was very Balinese, with much emphasis on hand

and finger movement, the cocking of the head to one side, and circles performed while dipping the whole body, a fluid motion interspersed with firm foot planting and total but brief immobility. There was little variation apparent to our untutored eyes and ears in either the rhythm or cadence.

Then, they – and we – were treated to a grotesque intrusion on their traditions. Nemesis, resplendent in an ill-fitting lime-green jogging suit and immaculate Adidas, grabbed a protesting Daku and forced her to join the dance then in progress. To compound the tastelessness, and to heighten the discomfort of all, Nemesis herself decided to join in. Unfortunately, she was exquisitely uncoordinated and totally devoid of grace. With her feet categorically refusing to answer the commands of her brain, she completely failed to follow the not-too-difficult steps. It was a complete embarrassment to watch her arms flailing, her vapid expression and mouth slack with self-importance.

Luckily, it was the last scheduled dance. The children then demanded that we, the representatives of the most advanced western nations, dance and sing for them an example of "English dance." A tolerable rendition of "Row Row Row Your Boat" was well-received after, by mutual consent, we let the endless refrain die a natural death. They seemed impressed with a lusty version of "Waltzing Matilda," the words to the second verse delivered with less than conviction, even by the Australians. But so far, no dancing.

A jazz recording of Bach provided the music for Nemesis's pièce-de-résistance. She had decided it would be all right to "jitterbug, because it doesn't matter what we do." Her pinwheeling through space was truly terrifying. We were stunned, shocked in mortification, and the young dancers looked desperately for a graceful way out. To think that this might be their lasting impression of the West!

Gillian saved the day. Although everyone had gotten to know a fair amount about each other, obviously there were still many unknowns about every individual's past. To the complete surprise of all the non-Canadians, she stood and demurely announced that she would sing a melody of a lovely girl. With a voice trained on the stage of the British music halls, she unleashed a spectacular outpouring of Maria's beautiful "I Feel Pretty," from *West Side Story*. The children were captivated, the sherpas dumb-struck and the trekkers incredulous. The applause came right from the heart, and the joy in the faces of the children allowed us to heave a collective sigh of relief that our final message was one of talent and of happiness. Nemesis, however, had been up-staged. Barging into the adulation, she asked frostily, "When did *you* do *Oklahoma*?"

The entertainment concluded with a mass distribution of ball-point and felt-tipped pens, pencils and balloons. Dick and Kendall examined a small boy (who turned out to be 17-years-old) with a tubercular hip which had stunted the growth of one leg by four inches. He was condemned to drag himself around in a crouched gait with an exaggerated limp. Walking around in this kind of terrain is cruel enough at the best of times. With his extra handicap life would be a living hell. The necessary operation would have been relatively simple, the leg could be straightened, and a built-up shoe could be worn. But who could, would, or should assume the responsibility and the costs?

And so to bed, to sleep for the last time in my sleeping bag.

October 21 – Day twelve of the trek – The four and a half pounds of eider-down in my sleeping bag guaranteed protection down to 40° below. It was overkill for the relatively low altitude and high temperatures. It was as if I had slept in a sauna. I awoke even before Sonam's call for tea, and out the window I saw a breathtaking alpine glow catching the low

hills behind the village and the little Buddhist temple nestled in a glade just across the rockgirt fields. The sun's rays fired one or two diminutive clouds overhead against the pristine blue of the sky. Beyond the surrounding hills through whose jungle cloaks we had passed we could see the tips of the highest snowcapped peaks. This, our last morning, was the first to dawn perfectly. Obviously, there was no justice.

We posed for the inevitable group portraits on the dewy lawn, and then walked the last half mile down the boulder-strewn path, past a tiny lake fringed with lush bamboo and ferns, to the waiting cars. By 8:30 the farewells had been said to those sherpas and porters we would not be seeing again. Then, bathed in brilliant warm sunlight that had been denied us during the entire trek at altitude, our motorized convoy headed down the road to Pemayangtse and Gangtok. The road was as bad as any in the world, and it was a frustrating prospect to spend the entire day in the car retracing our steps when a sign indicated that Darjeeling lay only 13 kilometers away down another turn. Our government-imposed itinerary demanded our 120 kilometer return to Gangtok, and over-night stay, then back out to Darjeeling via the same route by which we had entered. The rationale, of course, was to increase tourist spending. We would have been charged for the hotel at Pemayangtse on the way in even if we had not stayed there. So, a bureaucratic decision lengthened our trip by car by two full days.

The drive was a terrible abuse of our bodies. Too cramped to move, we endured every pot hole, wash-out and trans-verse canyon in the intermittently paved road. Despite the bone-jarring discomfort, the fumes, and the stifling heat, the trip was spectacular. The waterfalls were less powerful than they had been a couple of weeks previously, but more flowers seemed to be in bloom. The jungle was radiantly lush in the sun, but the thought crossed my mind that the

steppe Eagle
Aquila rapax nipalensis
(above: 2nd year, ventral view)

uninterrupted green, all year long, might begin to pale in impact, and to become perhaps even obsessive. The bird life was marvellous, and gigantic butterflies eluded our grasp.

At a rest point, our attention was caught by a haunting "kee-kee, kee-kee" drifting down from above. On wings that seemed never to flap, a giant steppe eagle, in second year plumage, soared a thousand feet over our heads, effortlessly spanning the endless ridges and spurs of the valleys that stepped away to our final destination. The thought came to several of us simultaneously that our escape would be so easy, so thrilling, and so fast if we had had hang gliders. This eagle was not interested in us and continued on his way. One of his fellows, however, had expressed considerable curiosity in a 1970s Everest expedition at over 26,000 feet.

At this same spot we watched two peregrine eyesses tumbling and grappling in play just at eye level not 50 yards off the road, honing those skills that would someday be needed, in the void which plunged three thousand feet straight down. Our road was cut into the side of a cliff. Recent road repair was evident, and we wondered when the next rock slide would occur.

We passed through Pemayangtse before noon, and could look back over the four valleys to Yuksam where we had trekked that first day. Then down the disaster of a road – boulders twice to three times the size of the car had fallen apparently straight from the sky, and had knocked out whole sections of questionable engineering – back down to the beginning of the terracing and the million shades of green, one of which was the shade we felt as the springs of the car had by now failed completely.

We stretched our limbs in the village of Legship which consisted of a main street lined with contiguous shops all dispensing "Famous Sikkimese Whisky" and an exotic delight, Sikkimese musk brandy. (My bottle was packed in my sleep-ing bag for protection, much to the surprise of someone at the dry cleaners who pinched it back in Montreal. I never got to taste a drop.)

Sitting on the steps of a small shop was a madonna-like young girl, certainly not more than 15-years-old. Pendulous gold ornaments and gold discs adorned her nose, but her greatest treasure lay at her side, concealed in a rectangular wicker basket. Her cherubic baby slept peacefully despite the fact that his eyes were covered in flies. A yellow-robed fakkir lotused in the sun, and small boys begged plaintively not for money or candy but for pens. A crudely lettered slogan on a wall exhorted all to "Vote for Horse," one of the political parties contesting this or some past election.

After eight and a half hours we rolled into the honking, bustling, spitting main square of Gangtok, past sidewalk vendors, and a row of squatting cobblers whose raw materials for shoes were abandoned rubber tires. The innkeeper of the Tashi Delek was waiting with white scarves to drape around our weary necks as befitting honoured guests.

At 4:56 P.M. exactly, my climbing boots came off for the last time, and exhausted and battered, I climbed into clean, dry sheets and slept an hour until 6 P.M. At 6:05 I made use of clean, odourless, comfortable, vitreous modern plumbing, and then soaked in a steaming tub for an hour and fifteen minutes. Surely this must be an anticipation of heaven. I washed the acrid smoke of countless cooking fires out of my hair and beard, and changed into clean, fresh-smelling clothes in anticipation of a monster feast in celebration of our return. An unexplained delay in the kitchen for over an hour turned anticipation and hunger into surliness and nausea. A dozen arrowroot biscuits and several bottles of Limca and Gold Spot prevented us from passing out. Finally, an endless procession of dishes appeared, and belatedly some tall sections of tomba.

Sleep now became our prime concern. A quick walk on

the terrace roof confirmed that the stars were as spectacular as ever, then down the flights of stairs to our rooms. The locals, however, were celebrating the anniversary of Buddha's birthday, the Sikkimese New Year, by setting off a battery of fireworks every few seconds. This joyous occasion lasted all night. We learned that the rather diseased-looking habit of pasting white or coloured grains of rice on foreheads in patterns devoid of apparent artistry was another way of celebrating. It certainly would have been quieter. To add to the sleeplessness of the night, the hotel was filled with holiday makers up from West Bengal. They insisted on playing their portable record-players at adolescent decibel levels endlessly through the thin walls. There is obviously something to be said for the solitude of the high mountains.

October 22 – The day dawned bright and clear, but clouds obscured much of the Kangchenjunga massif, obliterating much of the view we had seen that first morning at sunrise. At eye-level, out over the valley, a long-legged buteo (*Buteo rufinus*) sculled by on strong wings. Down below, the public toilets and showers were already in use, and the Lal Market was humming, banging, clanging in activity. Goats foraged, parriah dogs yelped and slunk away from a well-aimed kick, and another day no different from those before or those to come had started. The timelessness of the market scene was marred only by those corrugated tin roofs. What a mistake.

The shops were open along to the main square and I tried to bargain with a gold dealer for two beautiful torques. Their extremities were surmounted by heads of horned beasts. It was a design that is still in use, even though it pre-dated history. The price, I claimed, was absurdly high. I had no idea if it was or was not, but according to my instructions, everyone is supposed to haggle, the merchant would roll his eyes, be offended, and finally a compromise would be struck. This merchant followed another set of rules. He not only

would not budge, he also closed his shop, despite the fact that I showed signs of weakening. The torques were beautiful, and would have been taken for masterpieces created by Zolotas. But, as they say in Spanish, I had "disgracia con suerte." The bad luck was that I would not get those two torques, the good luck was that I would find almost identical bangles in Darjeeling at less than half the price. Gold in Gangtok is no bargain.

Disgruntled, I went back to the hotel for breakfast and sketched the bizarre blossom of the Bird of Paradise Plant on my table while I waited for tea, porridge and eggs to arrive.

The morning would be spent trying to inject some hard currency into the local economy. This would entail a visit to the Gangtok branch of the State Bank of India. What transpired was as much an education as had been the market. Commerce in Sikkim – and India throughout – is conducted in ways that are strange. It took over one hour to convert travellers' cheques into rupees, those priceless bills that obviously are the envy of the world. The main holdup – a bad choice of words: a not-too-alert armed guard stood at the door with a very large shot gun. Had there been a holdup, his shot would have killed everyone in the place – the main holdup was the need to enter by hand every serial number of every cheque and American dollar into two folio-sized ledgers, extracted from a teetering pile of them at random. There was nothing on the spine to indicate a date, hence whatever useless information was being entered would remain safely useless forever, for there was no way of retrieving the entries chronologically or any other way. Our disbelief at this institutionalized refusal to join the twentieth century reached the breaking point when a clerk rearranged 15 sequentially numbered travellers' cheques and began writing each 10-digit serial number out in full. I appealed to the short, owl-faced manager who had been spending endless oriental minutes

Tree sparrow
(*Passer montanus*)

Jungle
mynah
(*Acridotheres fuscus*)

Hill Mynah
(*Gracula religiosa*)

in deep contemplation of the mysteries of re-inking his ink pad, snapping his fingers for flunkies without even looking up. When we asked why the clerk did not follow the most obvious shortcuts, he imperiously squeaked: "This is our system. We are not computers, we are HUMANIANS, Sir!"

With the precious slip of paper now duly smudged with his over-inked pad, we were sent to the back of the line, behind the entire Indian army who had crowded 300-strong into the tiny bank. Our large brass tag finally was called, and we peered through the brass bars of a dark cage at an emotionless face that, upon comparing signatures on the cheques with those in the passports, decided that the signatures did not match enough and would not, therefore, give us any money. Had we been at altitude, our group would have fought each other for the right to strangle this twirp. A bellow shocked him from his smug authority, and he quickly handed over the money. Dripping with sweat, we escaped to the main square in search of a treasure to buy.

I passed up three human thigh bones with skin still attached to the upper joint, because I had no drums stretched with human skin to beat. And my son, Gordon, will never receive the pious drinking vessel, fashioned from the cranium of a deceased monk, lined with hand-beaten silver, and with a large lump of lapis lazuli embedded at the bottom of the hollow. The sense of continuity in religious artifacts is very strong. We did, however, buy filigree boxes studded with semi-precious stones, simple braided and banded torques, coral necklaces and stunning beads of silver balls, glass, stone and ivory. And we bought boxes of Sikkimese tea.

Laden with our booty, we repaired to the hotel terrace, and watched the house crows, mynahs, and especially the lively argumentative tree sparrows (*Passer montanus*). We held these birds in special affection, for they have not here been displaced by the house sparrow (*Passer domesticus*). It was a subtle but welcome change, the same almost smug satisfaction I had felt throughout the Andean cities where the local dominant finch is the ruffous-collared sparrow *(Zonotrichia capensis)*. The house sparrow has taken over enough territory.

After lunch, a Chinese extravaganza, we loaded up the cars, jostling with the continuous oncoming convoys of Indian army trucks heading for the Chinese border, we bounced our way down to the valley floor, checked out through the check points, and examined giant spiders while officials blinked at our trekking permits, and the entry visas of the Americans. We, and the Australians, being fellow members of the Commonwealth did not require visas, only trekking permits.

The Teesta was a pale copy of the raging river we had known only two weeks ago. Frothing torrents and rapids were now replaced by bleached and dusty rocks, sand and silt bars, and messy banks. Only in mid-stream did the waters still run swift. The monsoon was no longer refilling the reservoirs, and soon the mighty Teesta would carry a meagre contribution to the Brahmaputra. We finally crossed over the last suspension bridge, and headed back up through the teak and river gum forests, past the scenic spot where we had first seen lorikeets and giant locusts and sucked honey from hibiscus. The trees gave way to rounded closely cropped bushes, and we were in the middle of the endless tea estates. Files of little girls and young women wended their way up the steep hills, carrying huge baskets, tumplined on their foreheads to the weighing stations where their backbreaking work would be converted in a mere pittance. But at least it is a job. For tea has not always been here.

The Himalayas provided the rhododendrons and orchids for the formal gardens of the British Empire and through them, the gardens of the world. But the economic importance of these exports pales when compared to that of tea, by far the most significant import of this – and perhaps of any –

Tomba holders at Yuksam –

region. Originally, all tea consumed in England came from China, the only place where commercial exploitation took place. All that changed in the 1840s, thanks to a fluke in 1829. In that year, a Whitechapel surgeon, Nathaniel Bagshaw Ward, inadvertently discovered that plants could germinate and sustain themselves in an air-tight glass bottle, even though the chrysalis of the hawk moth, the object of his experiment, died. At the height of one of England's most bizarre natural history crazes, he was soon growing more than 30 different species of ferns in his bottles even though his home was surrounded by the foulest pollution that the Industrial Revo-

lution could produce. Ward shared his discovery with George Loddiges, the proprietor of a well-known nursery at Hackney. Loddiges packed a shipment of plants in these "Wardian Cases" and sent them via sea to Australia where they arrived in perfect condition in mid-1834. Up until then it had been impossible to send meaningful shipments of plants over long distances because of the hardships endured on the sea, such as salt spray and weather, which killed off everything other than those plants which could be carried in seed form. The Wardian bottle potentially changed all this, but it took the repeal of the luxury tax on glass (a measure originally imposed during the Napoleonic Wars) in 1845 to bring the cost of glass down to a commercially acceptable level. For the first time, the tea plants could be imported from China, and were established as a cash crop in the foothills around Darjeeling. The Hill Stations took on a new economic importance, which, having broken the Chinese monopoly, had profound and far-reaching political impact. Ward's "Closely Glazed Cases" not only changed the drinking habits of the world, they also helped re-draw the map.

The clouds closed in as we climbed towards Darjeeling, past walls cascading with ferns. Their double leaves were up to eight feet long. The plants themselves were garlanded with a beautiful yellow flower, each blossom evenly spaced every 18 inches down a single vine-like stem. It was fun to speculate on the size of a Wardian bottle that would have been needed to grow one of these ferns. Up through reforested pines in their geometrically perfect rows which paid no attention to the lie of the land. Up to the local height of land at 7407 feet at Ghoom where we intersected the railroad line leading down the twisting road to Darjeeling. The scenery should have been beautiful, but we were in a swirling pea-soup fog. Our headlights picked cars, trains, people and animals as they emerged or faded from view.

Tea-Pickers below Darjeeling on their way to the weighing station

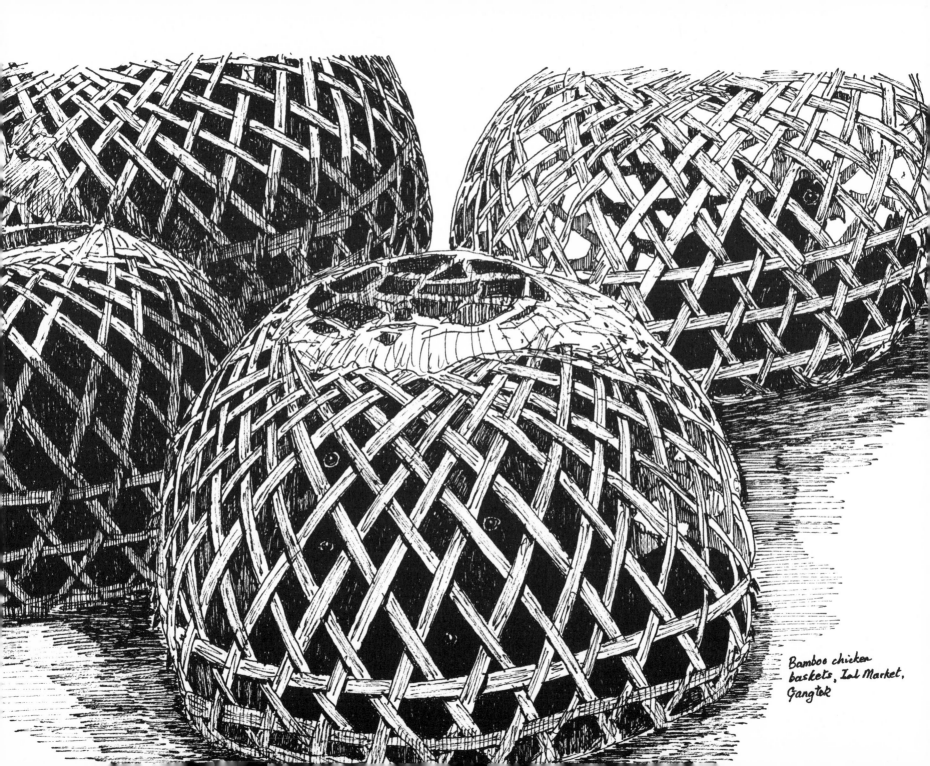

Bamboo chicken baskets, Lal Market, Gangtok

A little below the Planter's Club we came upon a jaunty, spry, athletic man with a red nylon windbreaker, matching red knee socks, dark glasses (in the fog!) and a tam o'shanter. Only the climbing boots seemed in place. I jumped out of the car, and introduced myself to Tenzing Norgay. The thrill was indescribable, not just of meeting Sir Edmund Hillary's partner, but also of meeting the man who more than any other – more than any government – has helped the whole sherpa nation to raise the level of their self-esteem. In delightfully-accented English he greeted Gillian and Mickey before continuing along the merchants' stalls, manned by refugee Tibetans, shaking hands, stopping to chat, and generally acknowledging the heart-felt and spontaneous adulation from his compatriots. We would be seeing Tenzing in his home later on.

In the rapidly gathering dusk, we bade farewell to our wonderful drivers, and trudged up the 50-yard inclined path which cut up to the hotel through the rounded shoulders of massed marigolds. The porters carried our duffles to our assigned rooms, we claimed our locked cases left here at the beginning of the trek, and we began the process of re-entering the modern world. Below the hotel, Darjeeling shelved away in a jumble of shops, bazaars, exotic noises and smells to the clouds and darkness beyond. Immediately below was a busy street with stalls abutting the retaining wall at the base of the hotel property. The clients, therefore, faced in our direction, haggling with unseen vendors for garishly coloured knitted goods in acrylic, plastic kitchen ware, and spare parts for anything and everything imaginable. In the gloom, all we could see were the swarthy faces that appeared as ovals of brown light reflecting the candles and kerosene lamps that extended business hours beyond nightfall. In the distance, the labyrinth of the city had taken on crisp detail under the almost full moon which heightened rather than

resolved the mysteries of this fascinating city. Tomorrow we would explore.

Before supper I spent almost two hours in one single shop at the foot of the hotel path. The walls were hung with unfamiliar treasures, giant leather containers for *chan* (the potent mountain beer) that hung from saddles; Tibetan masks with fangs and hair entwined with serpents; religious icons, and long trumpets; smaller Tibetan antiques overflowed the shelves and vitrines, and there was tray after tray of polished or rough cut stones. Most beautiful were the small bowls carved from the burls of hardwoods. Their marbled grains were lustrously polished to a deep chestnut, brown or ochre. They were lined with beaten silver and stood on a simple silver base edged in a repoussé frieze. I bought four, and Gillian bought three more while I anguished over a set of seven solid silver temple bowls of the same shape. Rightly, the merchant refused to break the set. The shop owner and his wife most hospitably offered us cups of tea with a faint aroma of rancid butter. With supper soon upon us, we could graciously decline, so to show their appreciation for our patronage they gave us small square boxes of silver with polished agate lids. Now that we had really culled the treasures we felt we could "share" our discovery of the shop with the other members of the group. After all, there are bounds to friendship.

Then, dressed up in our best bib and tucker, totally wrinkled after a two week confinement in our locked bags, we elegantly gathered in the cold and cavernous dining room. The waiters were all starched and stiffly white with persian lamb cadet caps and prominent brass badges with raised numbers far higher than four waiters would apparently warrant. If the numbers were to be believed, there had to be another hundred or more waiting in the wings. They obviously were not waiting in the kitchen, for the meal took forever to arrive.

Yet another perfect view
of fog-bound Darjeeling!

This unexpected free time allowed us to pay closer attention to the horns that sprouted from polished wooden plaques all around the walls just below the very high ceiling. When we had first stayed here, the trophy horns added to the atmosphere, but now that we had climbed in the native haunts of some of these animals they seemed to us to be a little sad. Here, blackened with age and with the oxidized lacquer with which they had been coated, were chirus, the Tibetan antelopes, considered sacred by the Mongols who foretold the future by the rings in the horns, and who considered the blood to have medicinal properties. When seen from just the right angle, the two long tapering horns overlapped exactly, giving rise, some claim, to the myth of the unicorn. There were the horns of tahrs, whose flesh was considered by the mountain tribes to be excellent for fever and rheumatism. And there were serows, ghorals, and takins, those strange Himalayan herbivores that seem to link the goat and antelope families. Some heads were fully stuffed, and stuffed incredibly badly. The ibex was so distorted that the horns seemed to have been arbitrarily stuck onto the head of a Himalayan wild goat. At least, hunting by the natives could be justified on the grounds of food or medicine or religion. But these blackened mementos of once vital creatures had been sacrificed on the alter of ego by bored imperial officers and gentlemen.

Sleep that night was a nostalgic vision of our beloved Reendesert, the family home at Bantry in Southwest Cork. Just as it had in Ireland, the tiles were cold to touch on the facing of the fireplace, which glowed forelornly with lumps of coal of no caloric value. The smell nevertheless reminded me of the peat fires in every room, and this more than compensated for the lack of warmth. I brought my diary up-to-date half-floating in the giant tub perched off the floor on clawed feet. The hot water would stay overnight to help

116

under a cosy, with toast, and a woven place mat on the tray.

OCTOBER 23. Darjeeling was magnificent under bright sunlight. Off to the right, the Great Himalayas towered above - far more so than at Gangtok. The architecture is classic Indian colonial. It's down at the mouth, but

Gerar - Shades of Reendesert! So this is where "Big Game Hunting in the Himalayas" and the host of others had been written.

these of many, in the dining hall of the Planters' Club, along with a vast collection of cricket cups from the 1880's "won by Squadron G" with the names that appear in the Memorial windows of the U. Club in Montreal. I know Col. Somerville was here.

OCT 23

-101-

give off the heat that the fireplace could not muster. As in Ireland, even the toilets were made by Shanks. The linen was heavy and held just a hint of dampness and mildew. The mattresses hammocked slightly, and the reflections of the sputtering coal danced on the high ceilings. Outside I knew there would be mistle thrushes on the dew-covered tailored lawns, and every dog that barked would be Sparky. Biddy Cronin must be downstairs cooking up rashers and eggs. The oh-so-subtle influence of the British Empire was as palpable in Bantry as it was in Darjeeling. At peace with the world I slept uninterruptedly for the first time in two weeks, until tea, delivered under a cosy, with a rack of cold toast, was delivered by the house boy at 7 A.M.

October 23 – Darjeeling was magnificent under bright sunlight. Cup of tea in hand, I stood at the rail of the balcony like the commander of some floating ship, and thrilled to the Great Himalayas that pierced the sky off to the right above an intervening spur of the city. Below, the city sprawled in its classic Indian colonial architecture, down in the mouth but still reflecting a faded empire. Braces of shaggy Himalayan ponies were being trotted up the narrow street for a day of carrying tourists around the square. Street stalls were unshuttering into life, and an early steam whistle announced a toy train behind the hills.

The morning was spent at the Tibetan refugee self-help centre where old men with braided hair worked with leather while women knitted coarse wools into rustic sweaters. Children played tag under the supervision of their teachers, and cooks prepared vast cauldrons of soup in a steamy kitchen. Above a display of samples for museum quality Tibetan rugs hung the local masterpiece: a four foot by six foot interpretation of the Skylon with Niagara Falls thundering underneath, all in the most awful tints, and – oh cursed luck – it was not for sale. This tour-de-force was, euphemistically, free of taste. And yet the other traditional rugs were of transcendent beauty.

On the way back to Darjeeling, we passed a little girl in a pink sari, kneeling by a spring to fill her water jug. Directly across the road from her, the hill sloped away thousands of feet, and off in the distance one majestic peak broke through the banks of clouds. It was Pandim, our sacred mountain. To think that we had walked there gave us a very special thrill.

There was enough time before lunch to buy carved boxes of sandalwood and ebony elephants, and for a visit to the Oxford Book Shop where a chance conversation with, of all people, a representative of Mountain Travel, was discretely overheard by the owner. Yes, we were indeed interested in rare books, and most certainly we would be interested in visiting his back room where his special tomes were kept. Here we found the first editions of Hillary's "Ascent of Everest", and of Tenzing's autobiography. Neither book was old, nor especially rare, but we were overjoyed. That afternoon we would be having tea with Tenzing, and would ask him to inscribe each volume for our assorted sons.

Then down through the endless bazaars, down through passageways that were more like stairs than streets, to a lower level of the city to a cubicle of a shop, devoid of signs and of displays. Surrounded by neighbours hawking chickens from radial bamboo baskets, here sat, cross-legged, the gold merchant in perfect anonymity. His inventory was in the safe, and the only tools of his trade consisted of a miniature brick oven and small vials for melting precious metals which were poured into cabochon-shaped lenses prior to hammering. He had two beautiful torques, similar to those I had seen in Gangtok, but the bracelet was twisted, not plain as had been the case in Sikkim. I made a down payment, and promised to return after a visit to the local branch of the State Bank of India. Luckily, today was an unannounced bank holiday, so we walked across town to the Mount Everest Oberoi where we cashed in sufficient travellers' cheques to make up the difference. Unfortunately, the hotel also housed a superb antique shop, and a fair amount of the cash was lost to spontaneous splurging. Back at the Planter's Club, Ms. Marigold was holding court in her amazingly cluttered office. A guest had just paid his bill, and a friend dredged up handfuls of rupees from a cavernous purse. There was sufficient money on hand for the wants of ourselves and several other members of the group. I mention this only to emphasize how very gracious and helpful Ms. Marigold was. With that kind of hospitality, she could be more than excused for having twelve Lhasa apsos yapping all over the place.

Gillian bought an inch-square slice of lapis lazuli the colour of the midnight sky at Pandim, mounted in a simple silver setting; Mickey bought beautiful beads, and I picked up the two gold torques. With the money that was left over, I raced back to the shop below the hotel to buy the seven silver bowls, but the shop was closed. I shall always regret not having yielded to temptation.

Then came the spiritual and emotional climax of the entire trip: tea with Daku and Tenzing in their home. Daku, dressed in her native finery, was a vision. She had prepared a huge spread of sandwiches, cakes and sweets for our whole group. Sonam and Norbu were there to help serve, and Norbu's wife was proudly wearing the Canadian gold maple leaf that Mickey had given her husband in appreciation for all he had done during her sickness. We sat and talked with Tenzing, who listened with real interest and affection of the days we had spent in the Galapagos with his earliest mentor, Eric Shipton. And he talked of Lars Eric Lindblad, and the Explorers Club in New York, and the wonderful experiences he had had throughout the world as a result of his having climbed Everest. His exposure, his fame, and especially

118

his literacy, had come quite late in life. His home was filled with the books that had been written by his friends and admirers, all of whom had inscribed appropriate thoughts. Tenzing said he could not read them, but he knew that the wishes came from friends, and that was what really mattered to him.

Among the clutter of his emerging taste and the outpourings of grateful statesmen and nations, there was one memento that struck us as being the most significant. Hanging on the wall in his sitting room was a framed portrait taken by the first lunar mission of the Earth rising above the curved desolation of the Moon's horizon. The astronauts, conscious of their own place in history at the pinnacle of the greatest technological support system ever known, inscribed the photo to the untutored mountaineer: "To Tenzing, who had seen great sights because he persevered." There was nothing from the Russians.

Upstairs was Daku's private Buddhist chapel, the most powerfully religious and personal place I had ever seen. A sit-up bed was laid should the Dalai Lama ever come, and prayer wheels rotated with the convection currents above votive candles. The walls were covered in glass-fronted bookcases with offering cups and other ceremonial paraphernalia. One jarring note was an electric tea kettle, a plastic thermos bottle and four or five large plastic picnic juice dispensers. Small prayer and religious flags hung from the low transverse beam; the back wall was lined with low, cushioned mattresses. The floor was of wide, deeply polished planks that felt soothing under our stocking feet. Orante Chinese red and gilt totally dominated the atmosphere visually from the walls to the more elaborate pieces of furniture. By our standards and canons, many, perhaps most, of the items in the room were devoid of taste, but certainly not devoid of devotion.

Outside, the fog had crept in, not on little cat feet, but on the piercing whistle of another train that scattered people, chickens and cars in its wake. The city had disappeared and only the sounds and occasional flickering halo of light hinted at human presence. Out on the flowered patio you could only stand and imbibe through every pore the timelessness of the moment as the realisation sunk to our very essence that a bond had been formed that could never be broken.

"I can write the letters," said Tenzing, "just spell out what you want me to write." With real determination, he wrote a message for our sons in his book, a message that he was unable to reread.

We walked back through the greyness of the clouds in a state of euphoria. I committed all this to paper in my diary while moving my wicker chair back inch by inch from a roaring fire in my room. The tub was running, and the clock moved inexorably and wonderfully ahead. Tomorrow, we would be leaving for Bogdogra and then home.

October 24 – Darjeeling looked out on thick rolls of clouds, sculptured into voluptuous blankets of greys and purples and blues. The fire had long since gone out and I awoke in the cold with a cold. Waiting for bed tea, I tried to repack everything – the treasures and films in one bag, the dispensables in the duffle, the fragile items in the small rigid and locked case. After breakfast we bade our new friends a sad goodbye, and climbed into a taxi in which the driver was incomprehensibly incompetent. His slowness would normally have been a saving grace, but we were already more than an hour late in leaving. He lasted less than a mile before swerving into an abutment. He looked truly perplexed when his wheels would no longer turn. We piled into Bruce's taxi, leaving our befuddled driver contemplating a broken axle. Bruce stayed behind to commandeer another car, and to follow with the bags. Kendall, Gillian, Mickey and I tried to make up lost

119

time on the corkscrew road out of the foothills down to the Plain. There was not supposed to be any time for photos, but two 1904 engines were taking on water near a trestle bridge in the jungle, patient passengers lolling on the roofs of the cars, or hanging out of windows. Nor could we resist a troop of rhesus monkeys, which, quite frankly, looked healthier and more alert than some of the spectres we had seen in Calcutta. What an irony that this species had been the first to be shot into space, a technological feat that belonged to a century that their homeland might never know.

Finally, down to the Plain, past lumbering ox carts, rickshaws, gaudy Public Carriers, with bangles and fringes cluttering the drivers' view. The heat was oppressive, the atmosphere shimmering above the brown bodies bent double in the rice fields. Paddy birds, white wings against sepia flanks, lumbered aloft, egrets posed above their reflections or hitched a ride on the back of a buffalo. Drongos by the thousands alighted on telegraph wires, tails extending far beyond the point of touchdown. We crossed a river, almost dry, its bleached boulder-strewn banks teeming with people, squatting under black umbrellas, hammering endlessly with small mallets to break stones into gravel. The sound of the countless hammers was unearthly. The back-lit clusters of humanity, the silt-laden stream, and the hazy green of the ditches and ponds begged to be photographed, but the plane would be waiting. It was, according to us, scheduled to leave at 1:30 P.M. (at 2:20 according to Kendall's ticket) and "some time this afternoon" according to our driver. The first announcement at the airport was for a revised departure time now scheduled before the arrival of the plane that was meant to depart. So we felt safe in having an excellent lunch in the coolness of the marbled dining room at the terminal. Outside, the air was sultry; the freshness of the hills already just a memory. The passengers were called, subjected to a rather thorough frisk, and ushered into a waiting room adorned with reminders that photographs were strictly forbidden. Off on the runway, out of sight, the reverse thrust of the Indian Airlines Boeing 737 announced the arrival of our flight. We boarded, buckled and at 2:35 P.M., we lifted off into the twentieth century.

Major Morton, once Deputy Commissioner of Darjeeling, wrote in the 1880s of Sikkim: "From the altitude of most parts of mid-Sikkim an immense survey of country is beheld. The deep valley of the Tista and its affluents, not more than 200 feet above sea level, lie below you, and from their depths you look up straight in one uninterrupted view to the summit of Kangchanjanga; so that deducting 2000 from 28,000 you have in one sweep of the eye 26,000 feet of mountain slope...in many places all over Sikkim. These and other circumstances, combined with the richness of the vegetations and botanical interest connected therewith, also the many kinds of beautiful birds—this mixture of scientific and picturesque interest—has rendered Sikkim the desire of everyone to behold...Anything more lovely, it is hard to conceive." A century later, Morton's words were still valid. That's why we went.

Kendall and the Macaques
on the Darjeeling-Bogdogra Road

121

EPILOGUE

We landed in Calcutta to discover that Air India's nontechnical staff did not care for the lack of fringe benefits, and had gone on strike. A speedy departure was wished upon the resident station manager, and to hell with the passengers. This development was of particular concern to us because the leg from Delhi to Bombay would not be functioning, and so we were sure to miss our connection to JFK. We spent frustrating hours outlining our predicament to the ground staff of Indian Airlines who frankly stated that they had absolutely no coordination with Air India, despite the fact that their offices were cheek by jowl. With the inestimable help of the ticket agent of British Airways, we determined that the greatest number of international flights would be leaving from Bombay, rather than from Delhi. It was imperative, therefore, that we get across the subcontinent post haste. Endless handwritten lists were consulted to no avail – our names were not on the manifest for *any* flight, despite the fact that we had booked, and twice reconfirmed our reservations. We finally arranged to fly via Indian Airlines to Delhi, and to be wait-listed on to Bombay, without knowing where or when our baggage would show up. Right in the middle of these very difficult negotiations, the public address system announced the departure of Indian Airlines direct flight to Bombay.

In stunned disbelief I asked whether or not there might just be some space aboard. Yes, there was. Why, I implored, did you not tell me that you were operating a service directly rather than waste everyone's time with the endless discussions? The agent, drawing on the same faultless logic as had the stewardess in the "nonsmoking" incident, blandly answered: *"You did not ask."*

After a short stop in Nagpur, we went on to Bombay where the entire transportation infrastructure of the country collapsed. Bombay airport at the best of times is beyond belief for institutionalized inefficiency, exacerbated by a peculiarly adolescent need for over-checking of personal identification. But now, under strike conditions, the word "chaotic" was redefined. Stepping over and around sleeping passengers and their friends, fending off beggars, trying to hold an agent's attention for more than a split second, rewriting vouchers, guarding bags, and paying exorbitant tips – all this required more mental effort and self-discipline than could be produced by any incentive other than self-preservation.

Flight 111 to New York would be leaving at 9:30, a mere five hours late. No rooms were available at the Centaur Hotel (we could see it in the distance, minus a few neon-lit letters), and the suggested alternative of sleeping on the floor of the concourse with everyone else simply was not acceptable. I merely refused to move until something positive was done. With the natives growing restive behind me, the agent finally relented, and handed over three vouchers for three single rooms at something called the Sea Rock Hotel.

Mickey and Gillian suddenly appeared and triumphantly announced that they had been able to book us three seats on the next Swissair flight to Zurich. As our excursion fare round trip was less than the cost of a single one way trip on Swissair, their good news would have cost us a mere 1250 dollars U.S. each. We would instead spend the night in Bombay at Air India's expense.

We reloaded our six bags onto a taxi with a roof rack, and agonized as our Sikh driver (and his brooding friend in the front seat), who professed knowing where the Sea Rock was, stopped two other taxis along the way to ask if they had ever heard of it. This must be quite a hotel, we thought. It was by this time past 10:30 P.M., not the best time to be driving down unknown roads bordered and littered with humans, asleep, sprawling, defecating, squatting in their hovels. The stench of human excrement surpassed even what we had experienced in Calcutta. The drive finally broke out of appalling slums into broad boulevards lined with palm trees and fine houses safe behind high walls and massive iron gates. Certainly this was the finest area we had seen in all of India. There were now few outdoor sleepers and even fewer sacred cattle.

Suddenly, we were beside the Indian Ocean, modest breakers surging silently against the rocky shore under a brilliant full moon. In front loomed a 24-storey resort, straight out of Miami Beach. Incredibly, this was the Sea Rock Hotel. On the top floor, overlooking the ocean, we sat down to a complimentary buffet to the accompaniment of the talented but ear-splitting western disco music of the "Dynamic Rosario Gonzales" group, dressed like John Travolta and amplifying out the best of the Bee Gees. Sophisticated and very westernized young people spent the evening bridging the two cultures. How selective the human mind can be: here was the latest manifestation of that detested western world which nevertheless the Indians fear to alienate.

For the 9:30 A.M. departure, we had been asked to be at the airport by 6:30. The night's sleep would be short, and we would get away before the antique shops in the hotel lobby would be open. This was lucky, for in taste and excellence the merchandise surpassed anything we had seen.

October 25 – At 5:30 A.M. the bell boy banged on my door (there being no phone) and a large light bulb promptly popped out of the wall fixture in the bathroom and bounced into my bedroom. We met for breakfast downstairs in a palm-fringed garden cafeteria, along with the crews from SAS and other international airlines. Then, with a spectacular sunrise behind a long line of royal palms in front of the hotel, we left by taxi. We could not wait any longer for the bell boy who had been sent back up to Mickey's room to find the walking stick that Norbu had fashioned for her prior to her

descent. With the flaming orange sky on our right and a still full moon in the pearl grey canopy on our left we headed through the awakening city to the international "interim terminal." Large flocks of egrets were fanning out to their watering holes, paddy birds solitarily flapping to their daytime haunts, house crows – many perched on the humps and heads of sacred cows – scavenged in their thousands. Uncountable hordes of Indians rose to face another day of hopeless existence.

The road to the airport was a broad divided highway, along which were spaced tall concrete pylons surmounted with huge discs. On these were painted the most attractive advertisements I have ever seen. All that was allowed was the company logo; the message was nothing other than a remarkably good painting of one of the Indian birds or beautiful flowers. There were scores of these ads.

By 6:35 we were in line along with thousands of others, inching imperceptibly along, kicking and pushing our mound of bags towards the agents who were not, as far as we could see, doing a damned thing. Exactly two hours and forty minutes later we had cleared the last hurdle, and with our precious boarding cards held tightly, we were frisked and ushered into the waiting room. The plane finally took off at 12:05. The seething, smelly, silly mass of humanity, their dogged refusal to grasp the simplest opportunity for sensitivity (the aged, crippled and infants were given absolutely no preferential treatment) and their resolute scorn of efficiency were as much a part of our cultural education as had been the villages, Calcutta's squalor, and the Lal Market in Gangtok. I could not recommend that anyone with a tendency towards hypertension or ulcers ever visit this afflicted land without having made prior arrangements for full-time help to handle all the details that spring up. If South America Andean states are considered the Third World, India must be the Tenth. The magnitude of the curse must weigh heavily on the educated expatriates.

As we lifted off, our wing tips seemed to brush the slums that were encroaching the very runway. Ironically, an air traffic controllers' strike had delayed our departure, just as the ATC slow-down at Dorval had opened the trip. We toasted our departure with a silent cheer, and welcomed the twentieth century with a cold glass of Veuve Clicquot Ponsardin Brut while the Indian Ocean rolled on in cloud-dappled furrows far below, unaware of the agony of its shores.

We made landfall over Oman, and overflew the tortured landscape of the mid-east. Plate tectonics have crumpled and folded the reluctant rock into what Mickey called a "papier maché" world. There was not a hint of greenery. The few scattered grey trees were limited to the wash plains of intermittent rivers. Judging from their breadth, these streams must run off incredible amounts of water in their season. Geometric villages, multi-laned roads, and Muscat's military airfields with feeder taxi strips leading to bunkers under the sand all spoke of oil riches.

The land changed from sterile baked grey to a definite rose as we crossed the divider between stone and sand. The "ocean of sand" is so appropriate. Vast, endless ridges, like the Pacific swell, parallel to the horizon were intersected by local dune patterns. The surface was brushed by dunelettes just as the breeze engenders small contrary waves and superimposes them on the overall surface of the sea. Most fascinating were the isolated and gigantic starfish-shaped dunes, hundreds of yards across and hundreds of feet high. With the aid of winds, they somehow move, spinning.

Then the coast of the Persian Gulf with magnificent shades of aquamarine, lapis, sapphire and white swirling together as the sands and the currents contend before the ocean claims them all. Far off shore, a small island with two storage areas like small caldera, a giant jetty poking a harsh tangent into the depths capable of accommodating LCBs. So this is what the world is willing to risk self-annihilation for!

At Dubai we made another landfall, now flat, baked, totally hostile, and yet there were many isolated villages and fields, walled off to isolate rather than protect them from their ultimate burial in sand. Even at 30,000 feet, the clear desert air and the binoculars revealed a wealth of detail. Then over water again briefly before flying in over Qatar and Bahrain with their absolutely vast tank farms, artificial harbours, jetties, booms and dinosauric supertankers. Installation after installation passed by under us. Iran was on our starboard, Iran dead ahead. We were flying a convoluted path up no-man's land to avoid the world's front pages.

As we approached Kuwait, breakers dissipated over perfect coral reefs which Darwin understood so well. Within sight were towering flares of gas, and a sea dotted with drilling rigs and production platforms. Then we flew down across a totally implacable expanse of brown, a dead world of sand, the true "Empty Quarter." We could even see the messy formations of nomads and their flocks; how in the world do they survive?

Every now and then there would be absolutely straight twin ribbons of asphalt, symbols of man's triumph over nature, but the edges were already blurred by the encroaching sand. Fleets of trucks and cars dot the desert as we approached the airfield. And tracks, like modern Nazca lines, point across the barrens in various directions. Pipelines were being buried, voluntarily or not, by the relentless sands. There was not a blade of grass. Wealth assumes a strange desert dress. We touched down in 100°F heat, and rolled to a stop away from the main terminal building. On the near horizon was a modern concrete city. Like the eye of a hurricane, nothing was moving, while the clouds of war swirled around us. We were not allowed out of the airplane, so we spent the 50 minutes getting caught up with those other Mountain Travel trekkers we had seen on the flight during the trip over. They, unlike us, had spent hours last night in Delhi airport before flying into Bombay at 2:00 A.M. They had spent the night under armed guard in the transit lounge of rat fame ("seized and pinioned and placed in durance vile" as they would have said of Hooker and Campbell in Sikkim in the 1840s.) At 5:00 that morning they were presented with rubber omelettes in a boxed breakfast. Our decision to bypass Delhi and to come straight to Bombay may have been one of the wisest moves of the entire trip.

We moved our clocks back three hours in Kuwait, and so we knew that we were really on the way home.

Based on our ground stop *The Birds of Kuwait* need not be written. A solitary pratincole was the only bird we saw.

Off, half an hour late, via Saudia Arabia, Damascus, Beirut, Istanbul, Bulgaria, Yugoslavia, Cyprus, West Germany and Belgium into the setting sun. We were exhausted, but sleep was out of the question. A totally grating six-year-old in the seat behind sounded like Donald Duck's nephew practising monosyllables. The alternative to a snooze was that wretched Sophia Loren movie we had seen on the way over. It was with a sense of relief that, having left some severe clean air turbulence behind, we began to feel the plane losing altitude. We flew in low over London with a nice view of the Tower Bridge, and the city ablaze with light. We landed beautifully, and raced to the transit lounge from where we dialed directly to Montreal, getting through in a matter of seconds. A tall glass of fresh milk tasted like ambrosia, and three strawberry yogurts were worthy of the *Guide Michelin*.

We took off at 9:50 P.M. local time, slept most of the way across the Atlantic, and landed at JFK at midnight. The clocks immediately went back an hour due to the change from Daylight Saving to Eastern Standard Time. We waited for hundreds of suspicious-looking travellers to be processed by immigration officials; we went through in less than three minutes. We collected our bags, went through customs and then waited for two more hours while Air India rerouted everyone all over the map due to the late arrival.

Then to a poor hotel near La Guardia, but at least there were no bodies, no cows, and no dung fires. Instead there were smooth roads, good signs and no horns. Supper was at 2:00 A.M., and then, blessedly, to bed after a drink of water straight from the tap!

Tomorrow was already today, and at 8:10 A.M. we boarded EA 770 for Montreal, thereby completing 60 hours of elapsed time from Darjeeling. And our record until then was perfect: at no time had a plane taken off or landed on schedule, and over half were not the flights on which we had been booked. At LGA the bags were handled expeditiously, checking was pure functionalism, the P.A. announcement was professional and clear, the intercom was faithful to the human voice. The sun was brilliant, America the Beautiful was never more so. *On time* we took off, and headed north over the onslaught of autumn's palette. Montreal was cloud-covered; the first break was just before touchdown and ironically, incredibly, wonderfully, the first thing I saw was the Town of Mount Royal and my own house! At exactly – to the second – 9:16, EA 770 landed *on time*. We were back in North America, in the twentieth century, and with our beloved families.

DML